DISCOVERING WASHINGTON

DISCOVERING WASHINGTON

Ruth Pelz

PEREGRINE SMITH BOOKS

SALT LAKE CITY

First edition
02 01 00 99   13 12 11 10
Text copyright © 1997 by Ruth Pelz
Maps and illustrations copyright © 1997 by Gibbs Smith, Publisher
Photographs copyrights are retained by their original owners, as
noted throughout the book.

Published by
Gibbs Smith, Publisher
P.O. Box 667
Layton, UT 84041

Cover design by Scott VanKampen
Interior design and production by Mary Ellen Thompson
Front cover photograph courtesy National Park Service
Back cover photograph © 1989 by Jeffrey High

Printed in Hong Kong

ISBN 0-87905-400-X

CONTENTS

UNIT 1

UNIT 2

UNIT 3

UNIT 4

Maps and Charts

ACKNOWLEDGEMENTS

The author and publisher wish to thank the following teachers who served as consultants on the manuscript:

Billie Jean Davis, Columbia Valley Garden School, Longview
Mike Fuller, Opportunity Elementary School, Spokane
Geraldine Jarvis, Hazeldale Elementary School, Vancouver

Washington's geography includes its towns and cities and the movement between them. (Port of Seattle)

Wild plants and animals are also part of the state's geography. (National Park Service)

INTRODUCING WASHINGTON'S GEOGRAPHY

This is a book about the place where we live, Washington State. It begins with a look at Washington's geography. Geography is the study of the earth and the people, animals, and plants living on it.

Geographers study many things. They study the location of places on the earth. In chapter one, you will learn how to tell exactly where Washington is located on a map. You will learn to describe our location in several ways.

Geographers study natural landforms and bodies of water. They also study features made by people, such as cities, farms, dams, and lakes. They study the climate. This information helps geographers describe places. Chapter two is an introduction to places in Washington.

Geographers also study relationships between humans and the environment. They study the movement of animals, people, products, and ideas. They use all of this information to help describe different regions of the earth.

This unit is an introduction to these important themes of geography. You will learn much more about each theme later in the book.

This photograph of the earth was taken from space. (NASA)

CHAPTER 1

WHERE IN THE WORLD IS WASHINGTON?

Have you ever wanted to travel in space? If you were an astronaut looking back at the earth, you could see that the earth is round. You could see areas of land and water. The large land areas you would see are called continents. The large water areas are called oceans.

Look at the map of Washington in the world. It shows the entire earth. Find Washington State on the world map. On which continent is it located? Which ocean touches our state?

WASHINGTON IN THE WORLD

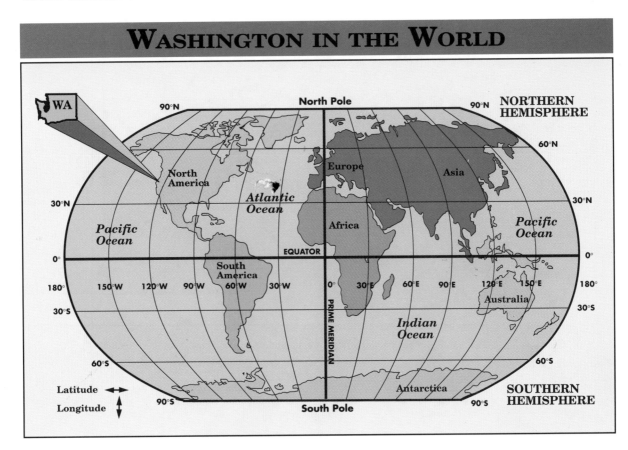

Describing Our Location

There are many ways to describe the location of Washington State. One way is to describe its boundaries. These are the lines that mark its edges. Some of these lines are made by nature. They are natural boundaries. Which bodies of water are natural boundaries of Washington?

Other boundaries of Washington are latitude and longitude lines. These lines are drawn on a map by people. You cannot see them on the earth.

STATE BOUNDARIES

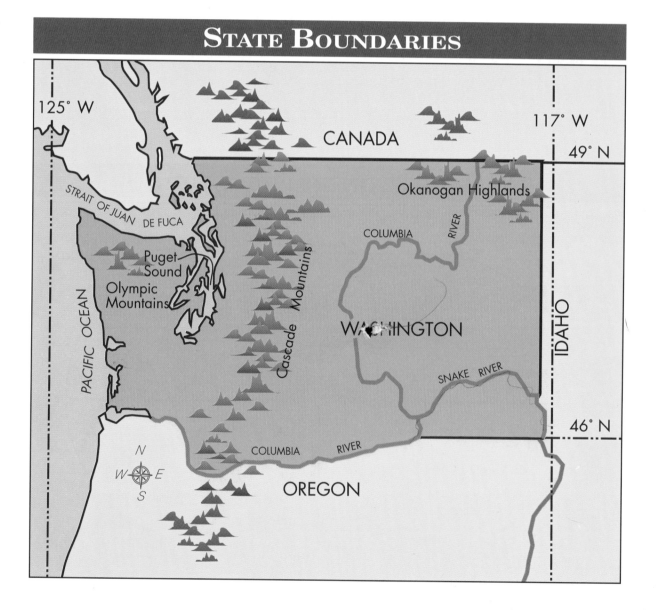

LATITUDES AND LONGITUDES

Maps and globes show some things you cannot see on the earth. The North Pole and the South Pole are two examples. Find these points on a classroom globe.

Maps and globes often show two sets of lines that cannot be seen on the earth. One set runs north and south. These lines all come together at the North and South poles. They are called longitudes.

The other set of lines runs east and west around the globe. They are called latitudes. The equator is one of these lines. It is halfway between the two poles. Other latitude lines circle the earth north and south of the equator.

All latitude and longitude lines are numbered. The little circle next to each number stands for the word degrees. The equator is numbered zero degrees latitude. The lines north of it are north latitudes. Where can south latitudes be found?

See if you can find the line that is zero degrees longitude. It runs through the city of Greenwich (GREN-itch), England. To the east of this line, you will find the east longitudes. They cover half the globe. The other half is measured in west longitudes.

Another way to describe location is to list the places nearby. (This is sometimes called relative location.) For example, Washington is north of Oregon and south of Canada. It borders the Pacific Ocean.

Location and History

Washington's location has been very important to our history. Look at the map on page 8 to help you understand why.

The first states of our country were near the Atlantic Ocean, far from Puget Sound and the lands of Washington State. There are two important mountain ranges between those states and Washington. They are the Appalachians and the Rocky Mountains.

The Rocky Mountains are the largest range in North America. Find them on the map.

It is not always easy to cross these mountains, even today. In the past, before there were paved roads, railroads, and airplanes, crossing the mountains was much harder. The land and people of Washington were isolated both by the mountains and by the long distance from other states. They were cut off from the rest of the country for a long time.

WASHINGTON IN NORTH AMERICA

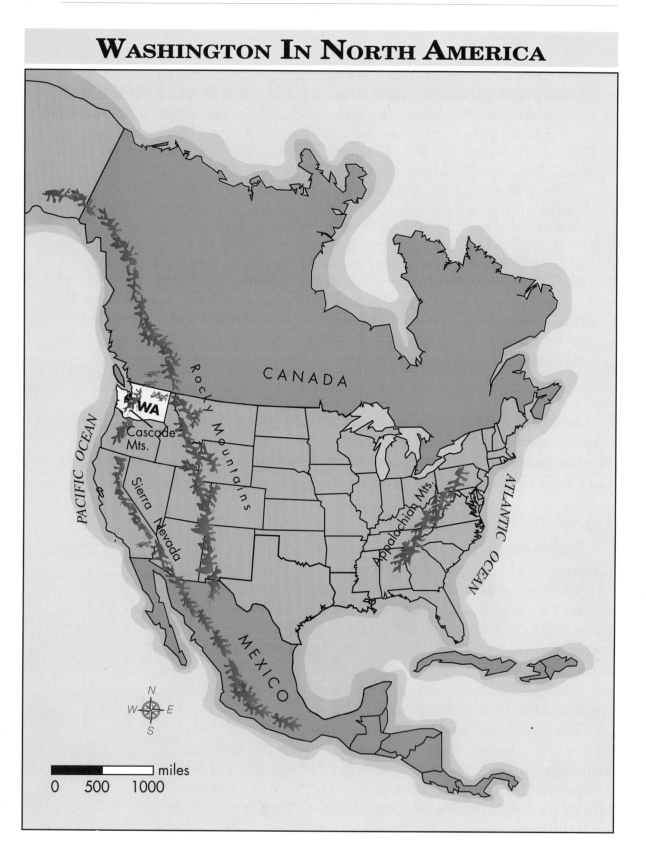

READING MAPS

Some maps show the whole earth. Others may show much smaller areas. This map shows just one neighborhood. Most maps have a scale of miles to tell you the size of the area shown and to help you measure distances. On this map, one inch stands for one-eighth of a mile. What is the scale of the map on page 8? How much distance is shown by each inch?

This neighborhood map shows streets, parks, and buildings. It shows these things with special drawings called symbols. The map key shows what each symbol means. Can you find examples of symbols and keys used on other maps?

Most maps also have a compass rose which shows directions. North is usually shown at the top of the map. Which side of the map is east? Which is west? Which is south? How can you tell? What other directions are sometimes shown?

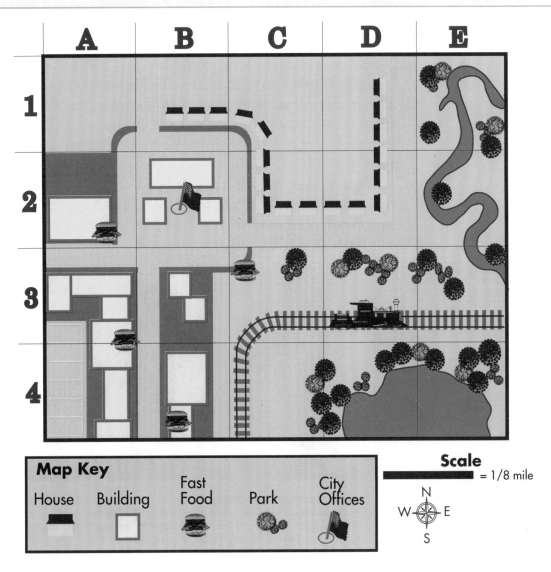

Map Key

House   Building   Fast Food   Park   City Offices

Scale
= 1/8 mile

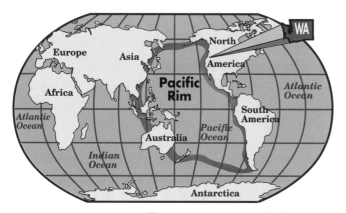

WASHINGTON IS PART OF MANY REGIONS

Importance of the Pacific Rim

Today, Washington's location is important in another way. Look at a world globe in your classroom. Notice all the states and nations located around the Pacific Ocean. All these lands are part of the Pacific Rim. (A rim is an edge, especially the edge of something round, like a cup.)

Each country around the Pacific Rim makes products that other countries want to buy. For example, the people of the United States buy clothing made in China and the Philippines. We also buy cars, televisions, and other products made in Japan.

Most of these products are shipped across the Pacific Ocean to the port cities of Washington, Oregon, and California. Here, the products are loaded onto trucks and trains and taken to other parts of the United States.

Today, many goods are transported in large metal containers. These containers can be loaded onto ships, trucks, or trains. Giant cranes are used to move the containers from one form of transportation to another. (Port of Seattle)

Many U.S. products, including wheat and apples from Washington State, also pass through these ports. The U.S. products are loaded onto ships and taken to countries around the Pacific Rim.

Shipping products into and out of Washington ports is one of the state's biggest businesses. This business is called trade. Trade with the lands of the Pacific Rim brings a lot of jobs to our state.

A view of the Rocky Mountains in Idaho. (Idaho Department of Commerce & Development)

Our Region, the Pacific Northwest

The history of Washington, Oregon, and Idaho are similar (alike) in many ways. Together, these three states make up a region of the United States. This region is called the Pacific Northwest. Can you guess how the region got its name? Study the map on page 8 again to help you answer the question.

The states of the Pacific Northwest have many things in common. They all have tall, snowy mountains and clear, rushing rivers. They all have evergreen forests and dry grasslands. And all three Northwest states have good places to enjoy the outdoors. People in these states can enjoy skiing in wintertime. In summer there are places to swim, boat, hike and camp.

REGIONS

The Pacific Northwest includes many smaller regions. Farming regions are an example.
(Washington State Department of Trade and Economic Development, Film and Video Office)

All the areas within a region have some things in common. Some regions, such as the Pacific Northwest, are quite large. These larger regions can often be divided into smaller regions. The Pacific Northwest includes mountain regions, forest regions, and desert regions, for example. It includes mining regions and farming regions. Each state can also be viewed as a region. The people within a state share a common government.

We can identify regions in different ways. Look at the area around Yakima as an example. This area is in a desert region. It is part of the Columbia Plateau. The Yakima River Valley is an important farming region. Each of these regions has different boundaries. You can look at maps in this book and in the classroom to see that this is true.

Where in the World Is Washington?

Word Skills

geography	continent	equator	symbol
location	boundary	degrees	map key
relationship	latitude	isolated	compass rose
region	longitude	scale of miles	trade
			similar

Things to Know

1. Pretend you are an astronaut, flying over the earth. Which of these things might you see? Which would you not see?

a. oceans
b. longitude lines
c. continents
d. latitudes
e. North Pole

2. List all the boundaries of Washington State. Tell which boundaries are natural boundaries and which were made by people.
3. What is the largest mountain range in North America?
4. What three states make up the Pacific Northwest?

What Do You Think?

1. Why are maps useful? Give as many reasons as you can think of.
2. Is location important to your community? In what ways?
3. Each pair of lines below is the location of a city. Use a world globe to find in which hemispheres they are located. Does any other place on earth have the same latitude and longitude as any of these cities?
   a. 40° north latitude and 80° west longitude
   b. 40° north latitude and 29° east longitude
   c. 20° south latitude and 29° east longitude
   d. 20° south latitude and 70° west longitude

14

Our state has many different kinds of land and water forms. The coastal waters attract millions of visitors every year.
(Washington State Office of Archaeology and Historic Preservation)

CHAPTER 2

WHAT KIND OF PLACE IS WASHINGTON?

The Columbia River crosses the Cascade Mountains in the rocky Columbia Gorge. (Washington State Department of Trade and Economic Development, Film and Video Office)

The people of Washington are lucky. We have a very beautiful natural environment. In our state, we have towering mountains and gently rolling hills, rich forests and grasslands, and wild animals of many kinds. We have long, saltwater coastlines and sparkling rivers, lakes, and streams. We have miles and miles of park lands to visit and explore. Our environment is one of the things that makes Washington State special.

An Imaginary Journey

Let's begin our study of Washington's environment by taking an imaginary trip across the state. Our journey starts near the Pacific Ocean.

We board our airplane near the town of Aberdeen. As the plane climbs upward, you see Washington's coastline. The northern **coast** is rugged and rocky. Thick evergreen forests come almost to the water's edge. In the south, there are sandy beaches. There are towns and farms and two large bays: Willapa Bay and Grays Harbor.

Now the plane heads inland. The Olympic Mountains come into view. The mountaintops are sharp and rocky, and the tallest **peaks** are covered with snow. South of the mountains you see gently rolling hills. Your journey continues east, across the Olympic Peninsula.

Soon, you cross a long, narrow body of water dotted with islands. This is Puget Sound.

WASHINGTON LANDFORMS

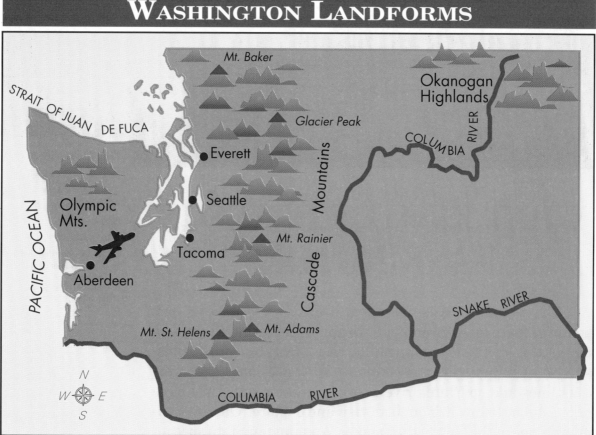

Mt. Baker is the third tallest mountain in Washington. (Washington State Department of Trade and Economic Development, Film and Video Office)

Along its shores are many big cities. Roads and highways crisscross the land. Beyond the cities, you can see farms and forests. This part of the state is sometimes called the Western Lowlands. The Lowlands area actually stretches south into Oregon. It includes several river valleys of southwest Washington.

Farther east, the cities disappear. You have reached the Cascade Mountains. These tall mountains rise like a wall that separates the east and west parts of our state. The slopes of the Cascades are covered with forests. The highest peaks are snowy all year round.

Five mountains rise above the others. Perhaps you can see one of them as you fly over the state. Mount Rainier is the tallest peak. The others are Mount Baker, Mount Adams, Glacier Peak, and Mount Saint Helens. You can read more about these mountains in chapter 18.

Sagebrush vegetation on the Columbia Plateau. (Washington State Department of Trade and Economic Development, Film and Video Office, photo by Sam Albright))

Hilly lands at the edge of higher mountains are called *foothills*. (Therese Ogle)

As you reach the east side of the Cascades, the land suddenly changes. It is much drier here. You still can see patches of green farmland. But you also see dry grasslands and rocky deserts. You have reached the Columbia Plateau. A plateau is a high, flat area of land. The Cascades are to the west of the Columbia Plateau. To the south are several smaller mountain ranges. The Rocky Mountains wrap around the plateau to the east and north.

If you made this journey across our state, you would see many rivers. The largest and most important is the Columbia.

It is the only river that cuts across the Cascades. All the rivers of eastern Washington empty into it.

For the end of our imaginary journey, we follow the Columbia River up through the northeast corner of the state. The land here is steep and hilly and still fairly dry. These are the Okanogan Highlands. They are **foothills** of the northern Rocky Mountains. There are forests on the high slopes, but they are not as thick as those along the coast.

We have reached the northeast corner of Washington.

Five Parts of the State

This imaginary journey has introduced many of the important land and water forms of Washington. It has taken us to five parts of the state:

- the Coast
- the Western Lowlands
- the Cascade Mountains
- the Columbia Plateau
- the Okanogan Highlands

You can find these five areas on the map. You will learn more about them in the chapters ahead.

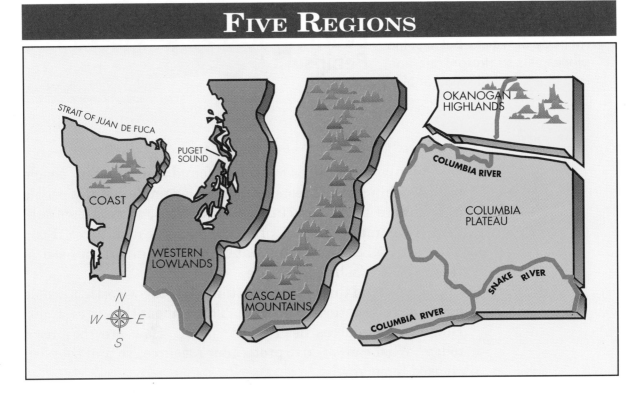

FIVE REGIONS

COAST PENINSULAS

There are two important **peninsulas** of the Coast. One is small and the other very large. Locate them on the map.

The Long Beach Peninsula is a narrow "finger" of land between Willapa Bay and the Pacific Ocean. As the name tells us, Long Beach is flat and sandy. Many people come to this little peninsula on vacations each year.

The Olympic Peninsula is much larger. In fact, it makes up the whole northwest corner of our state. Three bodies of water surround it, the Pacific Ocean, the Strait of Juan de Fuca, and Hood Canal. This last name is a little confusing. A canal is actually a waterway dug out by people. Hood Canal is a natural body of water. But in some places, it is so straight and narrow that it looks like a canal.

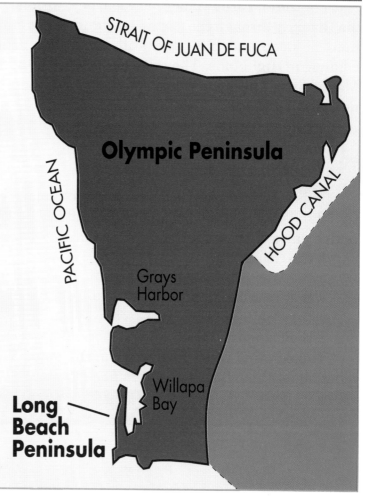

People Use the Natural Environment

Natural resources are things found in nature that people use. Washington's forests are a good example. Many people in the state have jobs cutting down trees, sawing logs into lumber, or making wood products such as furniture. Fish, minerals, and clear, rushing water are other important natural resources of Washington State.

As you read this book, pay attention to the ways that people have used our natural resources. Think about these questions: How were resources used in the past? How are they used today? What can we do to protect our resources so that they can be used tomorrow?

WASHINGTON: THE EVERGREEN STATE

You have probably heard Washington's nickname, the Evergreen State. The nickname comes in large part from our forests. Most of the trees in Washington forests are **coniferous.** They have cones, and they have needles instead of larger, flat leaves. Most coniferous trees stay green all year and do not lose their leaves in autumn, so they are also called evergreens.

These drawings and descriptions will help you identify some of the most important coniferous trees of Washington.

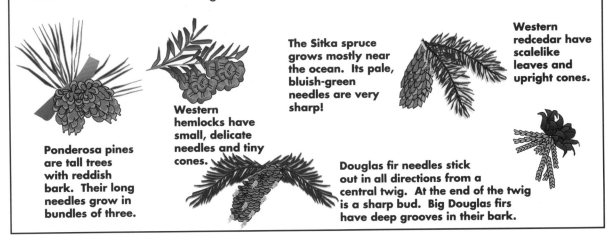

The Sitka spruce grows mostly near the ocean. Its pale, bluish-green needles are very sharp!

Western redcedar have scalelike leaves and upright cones.

Western hemlocks have small, delicate needles and tiny cones.

Ponderosa pines are tall trees with reddish bark. Their long needles grow in bundles of three.

Douglas fir needles stick out in all directions from a central twig. At the end of the twig is a sharp bud. Big Douglas firs have deep grooves in their bark.

AMAZING STORY OF SALMON

Imagine you are 500 miles from home. You have no map and no one to ask for directions. Could you find your way back to the place where you were born? This sounds very difficult, but millions of salmon do it each year.

Salmon are an unusual kind of fish. They live part of their life in fresh water and part in salt water. They are born in quiet pools along rivers and streams. They live in these pools until they are about the size of a finger. Then these young salmon swim downstream to the ocean.

Salmon (Seattle Aquarium)

They live in the ocean for three to six years. Then, somehow, the grown salmon find their way home. They swim upstream, jumping from pool to pool. They get bumped and cut, but they do not stop. The journey is long and difficult. They keep swimming until they come to the exact place where they were born. There, they lay their eggs and die.

Mountain goats' thick white fur helps them survive in the cold, snowy climate of the Cascade Mountains. (National Park Service)

Weather and Climate

The daily weather is important to all of us. The normal weather over a long period of time is even more important. This is our climate.

People can live in many different climates, but they must adapt. They must make changes in how they live. People in cold areas must build snug houses. They must have warm clothing and a way to heat their homes.

Climate is important to plants and animals, as well as people. For example, trees need a climate that is rainy and not too cold. Many plants cannot grow on the tops of the highest mountains, because the climate there is very cold.

The Climate of Washington State

Washington's climate has an interesting story. The story begins far out over the Pacific Ocean, and it moves from west to east. Most of the winds that blow over our region come from the west. As air passes over the ocean, it picks up moisture. This wet air blows over the coast and continues east.

Soon, these ocean winds reach the coastal hills and mountains. The air must rise to get over them. But as air rises, it cools. Cool air cannot hold so much moisture, so it falls to the earth as rain or snow. As a result, the coastal lands receive a lot of precipitation. Precipitation includes rain, snow, or other falling moisture.

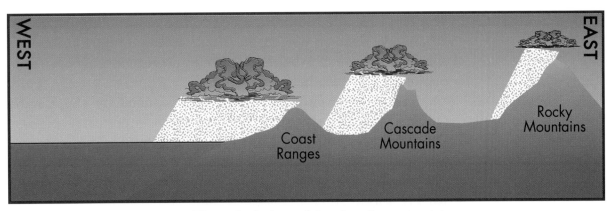

The story continues. The winds keep blowing from west to east, toward the Cascade Mountains. Again, the air must rise and cool. The west side of the Cascades is very rainy. Some parts of Western Washington receive over 100 inches of rain each year.

By the time the winds reach the east side of the Cascades, the air has very little moisture left. This is why the eastern parts of the state are much drier. Some areas are deserts. They receive less than ten inches of rain each year.

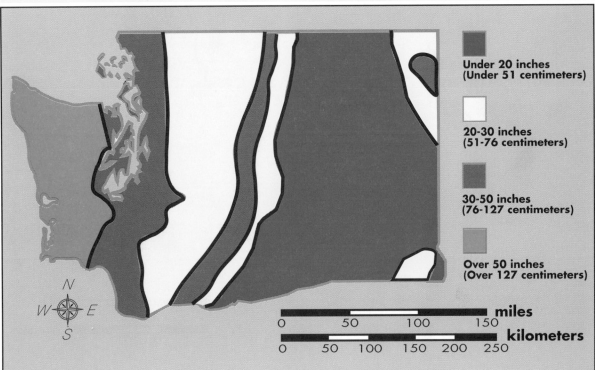

PRECIPITATION IN WASHINGTON

Under 20 inches
(Under 51 centimeters)

20-30 inches
(51-76 centimeters)

30-50 inches
(76-127 centimeters)

Over 50 inches
(Over 127 centimeters)

The Cascade Mountains divide the state's climate in another way. Eastern Washington has hotter summers and colder winters. Western Washington's climate is more **mild**. This means it is not too hot or too cold.

These differences in climate are caused by the Pacific Ocean. The ocean stays at about the same temperature all year. Ocean breezes help keep the coastal lands cool in summer and warm in winter. The wet and mild climate of western Washington is called a **marine climate.** (*Marine* means having to do with the ocean.)

The Cascades keep the mild ocean temperatures from reaching the eastern side of the state. Instead, eastern Washington has a **continental climate.** It is hotter in the summer and colder in the winter than marine climate areas. This is common in lands on the inside of the continent, away from the oceans.

ELEVATIONS

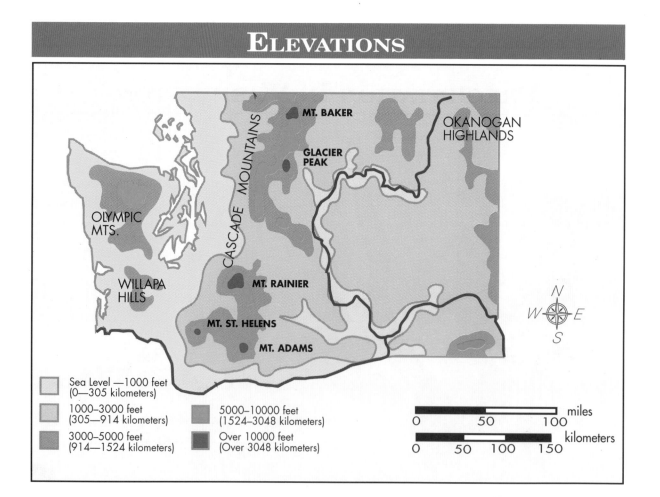

MT. BAKER

OKANOGAN HIGHLANDS

GLACIER PEAK

CASCADE MOUNTAINS

OLYMPIC MTS.

WILLAPA HILLS

MT. RAINIER

MT. ST. HELENS

MT. ADAMS

Sea Level —1000 feet
(0—305 kilometers)

1000–3000 feet
(305—914 kilometers)

3000–5000 feet
(914—1524 kilometers)

5000–10000 feet
(1524–3048 kilometers)

Over 10000 feet
(Over 3048 kilometers)

miles
0   50   100

kilometers
0   50   100   150

Climate and Elevation

We have learned that land closer to the ocean has a mild climate. Elevation is important to climate too. The elevation of a place is how high or low it is compared to sea level. (This is the level of the oceans.) The map shows the elevations of Washington State.

Literature

An Author Describes Washington's Natural Environment

The Egg and I is the story of a woman who grew up in Seattle. She became a chicken farmer on the Olympic Peninsula. These are two of her descriptions of the natural environment in which she lived.

Seattle Climate:

"In Seattle, the seasons ran together like the stained-glass-window painting we did at school where we wet the drawing paper first, all over, then dropped on blobs of different colors which ran into each other so that it was impossible to tell where one began and the other left off. Seattle spring was a delicate flowering of the pale gray winter. It was all over subtle and, as we wore the same clothes the year around, . . . we were never very season conscious. . . ."

Coastal Forests:

"The trees, some of them 8 and 10 feet in diameter, went soaring out of sight and it was dark and shadowy down by their feet. Thick feathery green moss covered the ground and coated the fallen timbers and stumps, which also sported great sword ferns, delicate maidenhair ferns, thick white unhealthy looking bushes beaded with fruit. The earth was springy, the air quiet."

(From Betty MacDonald, *The Egg and I*, New York: Lippincott, 1945)

What Kind of Place Is Washington?

Word Skills

coast   foothills   weather   mild
peak   peninsula   climate   marine climate
desert   natural resource   adapt   continental climate
plateau   coniferous   precipitation   elevation
sea level

Things to Know

1. Name the five regions of Washington. List three facts about each one.
2. Define the term *natural resources* and give three examples.
3. What landform divides eastern Washington from western Washington?
4. What is the largest and most important river in Washington State?
5. Which side of the Cascade Mountains gets the most rain?
6. How is the ocean important to Washington's climate?
7. Which part of the state has a marine climate? Which part has a continental climate?
8. Which lands are usually colder, lands with high elevations or low elevations?

What Do You Think?

1. What are the basic needs shared by all humans? Make a list and compare it with other students' lists.
2. Why is it important to protect our natural resources?
3. What natural resources are important to your community?
4. Would you prefer to live in a marine climate or a continental climate? Explain your answer.
5. How does climate make a difference in your community? (Think about the houses people live in, the jobs people do, and the way you spend your time.)
6. Most trees need more than 20 inches of rain each year in order to grow. Use the map on page 23 to help you guess where there might be forests.

CHAPTER 3

THE HISTORY OF THE LAND

Fast-flowing rivers change the land.
(Washington State Office of Archaeology & Historic Preservation)

The surface of the earth is always changing, although these changes are too slow for us to see. They take place over thousands, or even millions, of years.

Erosion is an example of slow changes in the land. If you visited the ocean coast or the Cascade Mountains once a year for your whole life, you might not see any changes. But the changes are going on. Every year, the ocean wears away a little of the land along the coast. Rushing streams and rivers also wear away the land. After thousands of years, the big rocks along the coast may all be worn away. River canyons in the Cascades will become even deeper.

Once in a while, the land changes much more quickly. The eruption of Mount Saint Helens caused such a change. Earthquakes may also bring sudden changes to the land. These fast and slow changes are part of Washington's geology. Geology is the study of the earth, of rocks, and minerals. It is the study of landforms and how they were made.

EROSION AND SOIL

The roots of plants help hold the soil in place. This slows down erosion. But when plants are cleared away, erosion may be very rapid.

This creates several problems. Dirt is washed into streams. This may cause flooding. It also may kill the salmon that need clear, rocky streams in which to lay their eggs.

Soil is a valuable resource. It takes hundreds of years for the earth to form the rich soils that plants need. Soil conservation is important to farms and communities around the state.

Inside the Earth

Geologists tell us that the earth is something like an egg. There is a hard shell on the outside. But inside the earth, it is so hot that the rock has actually melted. This melted, or molten, rock is slowly moving.

In some places, there are cracks in the earth's shell. Once in a while, melted rock comes up through these cracks, all the way to the surface. This is what happens when a volcano erupts. Molten rock that has come up to the surface of the earth is called lava.

Lava can erupt in several ways. Sometimes there is an explosion. Did you ever put your thumb on top of an open bottle of pop and shake it up? What happened? Do not try this inside a room. The soda shoots up and goes all over the place!

This is what happened to Mount Saint Helens in 1980. Lava and gas erupted from the volcano with great force. Rocks exploded into tiny bits of ash and shot high up into the air. We know there have been other eruptions like this in the past because much land is covered with old ash. The deep, rich soil of the Palouse Hills is a good example. It is made up of many layers of ash from eruptions long ago.

Sometimes, volcanoes erupt more quietly. Lava flows out like water leaking from a bucket, or like toothpaste being squeezed from a tube.

VOLCANO

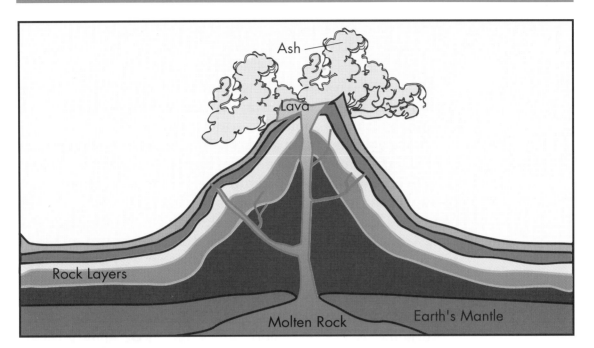

Mount Saint Helens erupted in 1980. You can read more about this famous volcano in chapter 18. This photo shows great clouds of ash exploding from the mountain. (U.S. Department of Interior; U.S. Geological Survey, Cascades Volcano Observatory)

The Palouse Hills area of the Columbia Plateau is one of the best wheat farming areas in the United States. Its soil is made of volcanic ash. (Washington State Department of Trade and Economic Development, Film and Video Office)

Long, long ago, such quiet eruptions buried the Columbia Plateau. This happened over and over again. The Columbia Plateau is the site of some of the largest lava flows in the world.

Building Up and Wearing Away

Lava and ash are two things that build up the land. Erosion is a way that land is worn away. All around the earth, the land is being built up in some places and worn away in others.

Have you ever filled a glass or bucket with muddy water? If you let the water sit for a while, the dirt sinks to the bottom.

Rivers and streams pick up bits of rock and dirt as water flows over the land. When water is flowing fast, it can carry lots of dirt and sand. When the water slows down, the dirt begins to sink. Little by little, over a long period of time, the dirt and sand pile up. New land is formed. This is another way that the land is being built up.

High in the mountains, you might see an interesting way that land is being worn away. The highest mountains receive lots of snow. Every year, more snow falls. As the snow piles up, it turns to ice. On Washington's highest mountains, there are thick fields of ice, called glaciers. The glaciers seem to be still. But they are actually moving very, very slowly down the mountains. As they move, they scrape the land. They pick up dirt and gravel. Glaciers can even move large rocks! Glaciers change the shape of the mountains as they move.

The Ice Ages

Over the last million years, the climate of the earth has sometimes gotten colder. These cold periods lasted thousands of years. They are called ice ages.

During the ice ages, huge glaciers covered the land. The glaciers formed in the far north and moved south. As they moved, they carved great valleys and scraped off the tops of hills. Puget Sound was mostly carved out by ice-age glaciers. So were Lake Washington and Hood Canal.

The last ice-age glacier covered the northern part of the state. It stretched south past Olympia and covered the Okanogan Highlands.

About 15,000 years ago, the last ice age ended. The climate warmed up again, and the glaciers melted. Water from melting glaciers caused great floods. These floods helped form the

Mount Rainier has more glaciers than any other mountain in the country. Glaciers form rounded, U-shaped valleys. Rivers often form steeper, V-shaped valleys. (National Park Service)

During the floods at the end of the last ice age, this was the location of a huge waterfall. Today, it is called Dry Falls. The river that once flowed here was many times larger than anything in the state today. (Washington State Department of Trade and Economic Development, Film and Video Office)

Grand Coulee and the rough "scablands" of southeast Washington. The small lakes and ponds of the Potholes area in central Washington were also created at this time.

The ice ages ended a very long time ago. But the changes they made in the land can still be seen today.

THE MYSTERIOUS MIMA MOUNDS

South of Olympia, you can find a very unusual landform. There are hundreds of low, round hills, something like giant pimples on the earth. They are called the Mima Mounds.

The Mima Mounds have puzzled geologists for many generations. How were they formed? Were these the home of prehistoric animals? Were the hills made by early Native Americans? Or were they somehow caused by the Ice Age? Today, most geologists believe that ice helped form the Mima Mounds. But they do not know exactly how this happened.

History of the Land

Word Skills

erosion	geology	volcano	ash
eruption	molten	lava	glacier
			ice age

Things to Know

1. Give one example of slow changes in the earth and one example of fast changes.

2. Tell two ways that volcanoes can erupt.

3. Tell two ways that land may be built up. Name two things that can wear the land away.

4. Where did the rich soil of the Palouse Hills come from?

5. Tell at least two ways that the ice ages helped shape Washington State.

What Do You Think?

1. Mount Rainier used to be taller than it is now. What do you suppose happened to it?

2. Why is soil conservation important to farmers?

3. In what places near your community is land being built up or worn away?

STUDYING WASHINGTON'S HISTORY

Were you born in the community where you live now? What things happened to you when you were a young child? Where were your parents and grandparents born? All these things make a difference in who you are. They are a part of your past, your history.

Our state has a history, too. It includes all the people who lived here and all the events that happened to them. We can understand people better when we know about their past. We can understand our state better when we know about its history.

How can you learn about the past? You can talk to older people in your family or look at old photographs. You can read books, old newspapers, and magazines. Old objects also tell a lot about history.

People who write about history study all of these things. They put bits of knowledge together like pieces of a puzzle to form a picture of our past. In this unit, you will be reading some of the stories of Washington's history. In the library, you can find other stories. Each one will help you put together the puzzle of our history.

The Ozette dig.
(Ruth and Louis Kirk)

A carved bowl from
Ozette. (Ruth and
Louis Kirk)

CHAPTER 4

COASTAL PEOPLE

Do you know what is happening in the large picture? Scientists and students are finding a kind of buried treasure. The treasures were made by people who lived in the village of Ozette long ago. These things made by humans are called **artifacts.**

Native Americans, or Indians, were the first people to live in the Pacific Northwest. They have been here for at least 10,000 years.

Most things made by the early Native Americans have rotted away. But Ozette is special. One day, about 500 years ago, a great mudslide buried the village. This covering of mud kept out air and prevented things from rotting.

Scientists have removed this mud very carefully. Underneath, they have found some of the old houses of Ozette. They also found boxes, baskets, and tools.

The scientists cleaned each object carefully and marked where it was found. With the help of older, living Native Americans, they studied every object to try to learn its story.

One of the things they found was a wooden bowl, carved in the shape of a man. (It even has human hair!) The bowl was used to hold whale oil. That is an important part of its story.

The Whale Hunters of Ozette

In the village of Ozette, no event was more daring or more dangerous than the whale hunt. The whale hunters were greatly respected.

They prepared for their task carefully, taking time to rest and pray. Finally, the day arrived. The hunters gathered on the beach. They boarded their large, beautifully carved wooden canoes and paddled out to sea. When they spotted a whale, the chase began.

There was no room for mistakes. One canoe had to come up close to the animal's left side. The chief hunter had to place his harpoon just so, thrusting it into the whale's huge body. Then the canoe had to move quickly away!

A second canoe came up from the other side. Another harpoon was placed. Now the whale was dragging two long ropes and many floats. These made it hard for the animal to swim and dive. When the whale finally tired, the canoes came in closer. The hunters killed the whale and pulled it to shore.

Everyone in the village came to meet the canoes. They gave thanks for a safe hunt. Whale meat and oil were favorite foods of the villagers. Everyone shared in the feast.

North and south of Ozette there were other coastal villages. From Alaska to northern California, wherever there was a mild, marine climate, these villages could be found.

Each village was different in some ways. The people had somewhat different customs. They spoke different languages.

But all of these Native Americans had many things in common. Today, they are sometimes called the coastal people. Their way of life was distinct from the native people of the Columbia Plateau.

The Importance of Salmon

Not all the coastal people hunted whales, but they all caught salmon. This large fish was their most important food.

It is hard now to imagine how many salmon swam up the northwest rivers each year. In a few weeks, people could catch enough fish to last the year around.

The return of the salmon was an important yearly event. When the first salmon of the year was caught, there was a special ceremony. All the people gathered to thank the salmon for giving them food. Then the fishing season began.

TOTEM POLES

One example of the differences between coastal villages can be found in their art. The most famous wood carvings of the coastal people are totem poles. Each carved figure told a story. Many poles told the history of a whole family.

You can see wonderful totem poles in many places in Washington today. However, you would not have found them here in earlier times.

The first people in Washington did not make totem poles. The poles were made in villages farther north along the coast.

Totem poles were carved by the coastal people of Canada and Alaska.
(Washington State Department of Trade and Economic Development, Film and Video Office)

Native Americans knew that salmon swim up the rivers each year. They also knew that salmon rest in rocky pools as they jump upstream. Native fishermen built wooden fences across the rivers to trap salmon in the pools. This Native American is wearing modern clothing, but he is still fishing the old way. He lifts salmon out of the pools using nets with long wooden handles.
(Special Collections Division, University of Washington Libraries; Collier)

The Native Americans knew many ways to catch salmon. One way was to build a wooden fence, or **weir,** across a stream. The salmon could not swim past it. A fisherman would stand beside the weir. With a spear or net, he could pull out one fish after another.

Some of the salmon were eaten fresh. Barbecued salmon, Native American style, is still a delicious treat today. But the rest of the catch would have to be stored away. The women of the village cut each fish, cleaned it, and removed the bones. The cleaned fish were hung on wooden racks over smoky fires. Smoking and drying the fish in this way kept them from spoiling. They would last until the next fishing season.

The Native Americans dried other foods, too. They spread berries in the sun. They made cakes from wild roots of the camas and other plants. These were dried and stored.

Of course, dried foods are not as tasty as fresh foods. Indian children liked to dip their dried foods in whale oil before eating them.

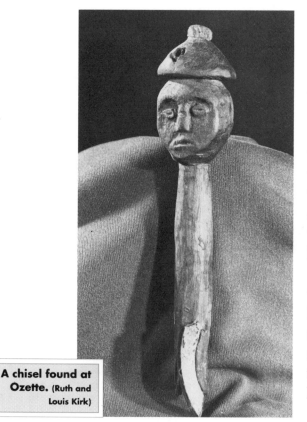

A chisel found at Ozette. (Ruth and Louis Kirk)

Skilled Woodworkers

Another object found at Ozette was a carving tool. It is made of wood and has a sharp beaver's tooth at one end.

Native Americans studied nature carefully. They saw that beavers could cut down young trees with their sharp teeth. So they used a beaver tooth to make this carving tool. They made other tools of shell, bone, and stone.

The coastal people were skilled woodworkers. They made wooden houses, bowls and boxes, masks, and canoes. They did all this without metal tools. And they made some of the most beautiful carvings in all North America.

THE WONDERFUL CEDAR TREE

Of all the trees in the coastal forests, none was more important than the cedar. The wood from this tree can be split fairly easily. Using wooden wedges, the coastal people split cedar logs into long, thick boards.

They used these boards to build their longhouses. First, they made a frame of cedar posts, set into the earth. Then they attached the boards to the posts. The boards were overlapped to keep rain from leaking inside. Each house was large enough for several families. Other cedar boards served as shelves and sleeping bunks. Cedar is a wonderful building material. It lasts a long time in the rainy coastal climate.

The people of the coastal villages lived in big, wooden houses. Usually, several families lived in each house. This drawing shows how a longhouse looked inside. (Special Collections Division, University of Washington Libraries)

Another special and very useful part of the cedar is its bark. The inner bark of the tree is soft and stringy. Coastal people used it to weave hats, baskets, mats, and even clothing. They twisted pieces of bark together to make thick, strong ropes. Cedar and salmon were central to the coastal people's way of life.

Culture of the Coastal People

The coastal people used many things from the natural environment. They gathered mussels, clams, and oysters from the beaches to eat. They also hunted small animals for food. They wove baskets from reeds and grasses. They wove blankets from mountain-goat wool and dog hair. They knew which plants made good medicines.

Native Americans had great respect for the natural environment. They believed that people were part of that environment and should live in harmony with it. These beliefs were an important part of their culture.

A culture is the way of life of a group of people. It includes the kinds of food they eat and houses they live in. It includes language and religion and the way that children are raised. It includes technology—the skills, knowledge, and tools that people use. It includes the way that people make their living.

Like people everywhere, the coastal people needed knowledge and skills to survive. The children in coastal villages did not go to school to learn these skills. They learned by watching and listening to the adults and helping them do their work. The children learned many important lessons through **legends.** These special stories taught children about the beliefs and history of their village. Through legends, older family members shared their knowledge and entertained the children on long winter nights.

POTLATCH

The coastal people had a special way to celebrate important events such as a wedding. The guests at a potlatch had an important role. They were witnesses who promised to remember and report what they had seen. Each guest received a gift.

A potlatch included a big feast and dramatic performances. The hosts performed songs and dances that were special possessions of the family. Often, people were invited from other villages to come and share in these large and wonderful events.

Potlatch hosts sometimes saved for years in order to have a large number of gifts to give their guests. Blankets were a popular gift item. Woven wool blankets like these were brought to coastal villages by the Hudson's Bay Company, described in chapter 7.(Courtesy Dept. Library Services, American Museum of Natural History)

This Is My Land

This is my land
From the time of the first moon
Till the time of the last sun
It was given to my people.
Wha-neh Wha-neh, the great giver of life
Made me out of the earth of this land.
He said, "You are the land, and the land is
    you."
I take good care of this land,
For I am part of it,
I take good care of the animals,
For they are my brothers and sisters,
I take care of the streams and rivers,
For they clean my land.
I honor Ocean as my father,
For he gives me food and a means of
    travel.
Ocean knows everything, for he is every-
    where.
Ocean is wise, for he is old.
Listen to Ocean, for he speaks wisdom
He sees much, and knows more.
He says, "Take care of my sister, Earth,
She is young and has little wisdom, but
    much kindness."
"When she smiles, it is springtime."
"Scar not her beauty, for she is beautiful
    beyond all things."
"Her face looks eternally upward to the
    beauty of sky and stars,
When once she lived with her father,
    Sky,"
I am forever grateful for this beautiful
    and bountiful earth.
God gave it to me
This is my land.

(Clarence Pickernell [Quinault], Taholah: Center for Indian
Teacher Education, *The History and Culture of the Indians of
Washington State: A Curriculum Guide*. Olympia: Washington
State Superintendent of Public Instruction, 1975.)

Coastal People

Word Skills

artifact   longhouse   legend
Native American   culture   potlatch
weir   technology

Things to Know

1. Who were the first people in the land that is now Washington State?
2. Who were the coastal people? Where did they live?
3. What was the most important food of the coastal people?
4. What other foods did coastal people eat? Give at least five examples.
5. Why was the cedar tree important? What things did Native Americans make from cedar?

What Do You Think?

1. The first people in Washington made everything they needed from the natural resources around them. Could you do this today? Explain.
2. What special skills did the coastal people have? Make a list of all you can think of.

CHAPTER 5

Plateau people decorated their clothing with beautiful designs. In early times, they used natural materials, such as leather, shells, and porcupine quills. Later they also used woven cloth and glass beads. (Special Collections Division, University of Washington Libraries)

A leather shirt, decorated with beads. (The High Desert Museum)

PLATEAU PEOPLE

At the time when people still lived in the village of Ozette, other Native Americans lived all over North America. They had different ways of meeting their basic needs.

Eastern Washington was home to the plateau people. Their culture was quite different from the people who lived along the coast.

Food was harder to find on the dry lands. The winters were colder and there were few trees. These things made a difference in the homes that people built.

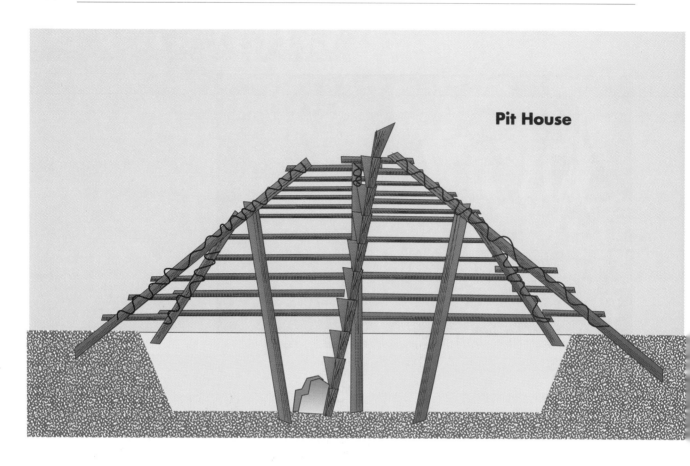

Pit House

In winter, the plateau people lived in snug pit houses, built partly into the earth. First, the families dug a large pit, a few feet deep. Then they leaned poles together across the top. Leaves and brush were laid over the poles. Finally, earth was packed onto this roof. A fire in the center of the earth floor kept the house warm. A hole in the center of the roof allowed the smoke to escape. This hole also served as a door. People climbed into and out of the house using a ladder.

To keep warm in winter, the plateau people made blankets of animal fur. They made leather clothing and decorated it with porcupine quills. Later, they used beads for decoration, too.

The summer houses were made of woven mats on a frame of wooden poles. The houses were rectangular in shape, with rounded corners. They were cool and shady in the summer sun. The mats could be carried from camp to camp.

Fishing

In some parts of our continent, Native American people raised most of their food by farming. But the coastal and plateau people of Washington depended on hunting, fishing, and gathering wild plants. Each year, they traveled to several different locations to find food.

When the weather turned warm, plateau people left their winter houses and went to gather food. Spring was salmon fishing time. Each group had its own fishing spot. Many were along the Columbia River. The area where The Dalles, Oregon, is located was a favorite fishing and gathering place.

Salmon fishing days were a time for both work and play. There were horse races, foot races, and games to be played. There was also much visiting and trading with people from other tribes of the coast and the plateau.

Hunting and Gathering

In summer, there were trips to gather roots, berries, seeds, and other wild plants to eat. One of the plateau peoples' most important foods was the starchy root of the camas plant.

This modern Native American woman has been gathering food in the old way. She used a digging stick to gather roots. She will carry the roots in hand-woven baskets.
(Oregon State Highway Department)

Native Americans made arrowheads and other tools from stones.
(Washington State Office of Archaeology & Historic Preservation)

In addition to fishing and gathering wild plants for food, plateau people hunted deer, rabbits, mountain goats, sheep, elk, and birds.

The main hunting season came in early fall. Plateau hunters made arrows of wood and attached sharp stone points. They made bows from wood and leather or from the horns of mountain sheep. They made traps, spears, and other hunting tools.

Horses Came to America

Long, long ago, an early kind of horse lived in North America. But these animals became extinct. The first horses of the kind we know were brought here by Spanish explorers about 500 years ago.

Native Americans quickly realized the usefulness of horses. People on horseback could travel farther in search of food. They could carry heavier loads.

Horses brought many changes to the cultures of the Great Plains, east of Washington. In time, the plateau tribes also began to use horses. Then the men could make even longer hunting trips. They traveled to the Great Plains and hunted buffalo. A tribe's hunting and gathering lands might stretch more than 100 miles.

PLATEAU NEIGHBORS ON THE GREAT PLAINS

The best-known Native American cultures are those of the Great Plains. These vast, grassy lands lie east of the Rocky Mountains. They were the home of the buffalo.

The plains people were famous buffalo hunters. They ate buffalo meat. They used the buffalo skins to make tipis, which are tall, cone-shaped tents held up by a circle of tall poles.

Plains hunters wore leather leggings, shirts, and moccasins. They wore feathers in their hair. They were skilled horsemen. They are the Indians most often seen in movies and books. But they were just one of the Native American cultures in North America.

Horses allowed the plateau people to visit the Great plains and trade with the people there. This trade brought changes to plateau culture.

Plateau people learned from their neighbors on the Great Plains how to make tipis. Plateau clothing also began to change. (Oregon State Highway)

Plains people moved their belongings from place to place using tipi poles to make a travois (trav-WAH). This is another skill the plateau tribes learned to use. (Special Collections Division, University of Washington Libraries)

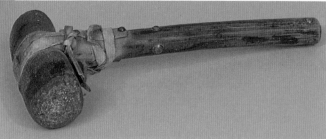

This basket and hammer were made by the plateau tribes.
(Courtesy of the Thomas Burke Memorial, Washington State Museum, Catalog Numbers 2-1834, 4962)

Some of the plateau tribes became very skilled at raising horses. For example, the famous Appaloosa horses were named for the Palouse tribe who raised them. (The Palouse Hills were named for the same people.) A cowboy sometimes called his horse "my old cayuse." Cayuse is the name of another plateau tribe.

Plateau Children

Like the Native American children of the coast, plateau children learned about their culture by helping adults. Boys learned to hunt and to make tools. Girls learned how to gather camas roots and other plants. They also learned how to weave beautiful baskets.

Native Americans were careful observers of nature. Some of the children's favorite games came from the animals they saw. In a "crab race," coastal children got down on their hands and knees and raced sideways, like crabs. In a "bear race," they had to move like bears. First the right arm and right leg went forward, then the left arm and left leg. Try this sometime. It takes practice!

Here is a part of one legend which the plateau children enjoyed.

How Coyote Made the Indian Tribes

Long ago, when animals walked the earth like people, a giant beaver monster named Wishpoosh lived in Lake Cle Elum. Lake Cle Elum was full of fish, enough fish for all the animal people. But Wishpoosh would not let the people get any fish. Whenever people came to the lake, Wishpoosh killed them.

The animal people begged Coyote, who was very clever, to help them. Coyote agreed. But he knew that other animals had tried to kill Wishpoosh and failed. What could he do?

Coyote's sisters gave him an idea. He tried it. Coyote made a huge spear and tied it to his wrist. He went to the lake and began to fish. Of course, Wishpoosh saw him and attacked.

Coyote drove the spear into the monster's side. Wishpoosh roared with pain and dove to the bottom, pulling Coyote with him. The two animals fought long and hard. They fought so hard that they tore great holes in the earth. One long hole became the Yakima River. The other became the Columbia River.

Finally, Coyote tricked the monster and killed him.

"From your body, mighty Wishpoosh, I will make a new race of people," said Coyote. He made the Klickitat people from the monster's legs. "You shall be famous runners and great horsemen," he said. Coyote made the Cayuse people from the arms of the monster. "You shall be powerful with bows and arrows and war clubs." From the ribs, he made the Yakima people. "You shall be the helpers and protectors of the poor people," said Coyote. From the head, he created the Nez Perce tribe. "You shall be people of intelligence. You will also be skillful horsemen and brave warriors."

Tribal Leaders

Among plateau cultures there was little difference between rich and poor. Decisions were made by a group of respected leaders. These were often people with special skills in one area. For example, one person might lead the others in hunting. A brave and skilled fighter might become the tribe's leader in war.

One kind of leader in both coastal and plateau tribes was the shaman. Shamans were religious leaders, who also had the job of curing the sick. Native Americans believed that all things had spirits. They believed these spirits could sometimes cause diseases. They believed that sick people needed a cure for both the body and the spirit.

Shamans were people with special power over spirits. They used medicines made from plants to heal people. They also used special spirit songs and dances.

Native Americans treated older people with great respect. This is how an early visitor described his experience in a plateau village:

"I observed an old woman in one of the lodges which I entered. She was entirely blind, as I was informed by signs, and had lived more than 100 winters. She occupied the best position in the house, and when she spoke, great attention was paid to what she said." (From the journals of Lewis and Clark)

Plateau People

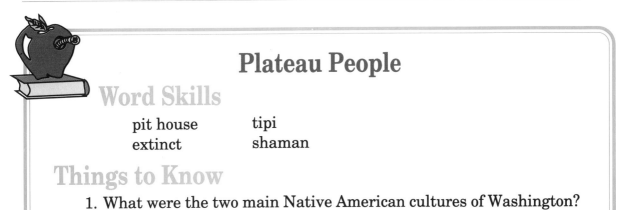

Word Skills

pit house   tipi
extinct   shaman

Things to Know

1. What were the two main Native American cultures of Washington?
2. What kind of house did plateau people have in winter? In summer?
3. In what ways did the horse change the lives of the plateau people?
4. What was the role of the shaman?
5. What Native American culture is most often seen in movies and books? Where did these people live?

What Do You Think?

1. List two or three basic needs of all people. Explain how the coastal and plateau people met these needs.
2. If you could build a Native American house to live in, would you choose a longhouse, a pit house, or a tipi? Explain your answer.
3. If you could learn any skill of the Native Americans in Washington, which skill would you choose?
4. Plateau cultures changed through trade with coastal and plains tribes. Can you think of ways that our modern culture is changing through trade with other cultures?

The explorers traveled in wooden sailing ships like the one shown here. Many sailors were needed to tend each ship.
(Tom Darden, Historic St. Mary's City)

CHAPTER 6

There are big rocks like this along much of the Pacific Northwest coast. Why are these rocks dangerous to ships? Why do you suppose the explorers stayed far from land when the weather was foggy? (National Park Service)

THE EXPLORERS COME

Native Americans have lived in the Pacific Northwest for thousands of years. For most of this time, they were the only people here. Other people in the world knew nothing about this region. They did not even know it existed.

The first visitors arrived about 450 years ago. They were explorers. These are people who go to unknown lands to learn about them.

The explorers' journeys were long and full of dangers. But there were good reasons to make the trips. An explorer might find great riches. He might find lands for his country to claim.

The Spanish in North America

The first explorers to see the lands of the Pacific Northwest were from Spain. Florida, California, Arizona, Colorado, Nevada, New Mexico, and Texas were once Spanish lands. So were Mexico and all of Central America. Spanish explorers set out from California and Mexico to explore the Pacific coast of North America.

In 1542, Bartolome Ferrello became the first explorer to see the coast of Oregon. In 1774, another Spanish explorer named Juan Perez sailed up the Pacific coast as far as southern Alaska.

SPANISH MISSIONARIES

A Spanish mission in California. (Special Collections Division, University of Washington Libraries; Frank La Roche)

Christopher Columbus and many of the first explorers in North America came from Spain. They claimed much of the land on our continent.

Later, Spanish missionaries came to live in North America. They wanted to teach Native Americans about the Catholic religion and way of life. Native Americans attended the mission schools and churches. They worked on the mission farms and ranches.

Over time, the Spanish and Native American cultures blended. A new American culture formed. It is often called Mexican American or Hispanic. The people at the missions were the ancestors of many Hispanic people now in the United States. Today, large numbers of Hispanic Americans live in the Yakima Valley and other parts of Washington State.

EXPLORATION ROUTES

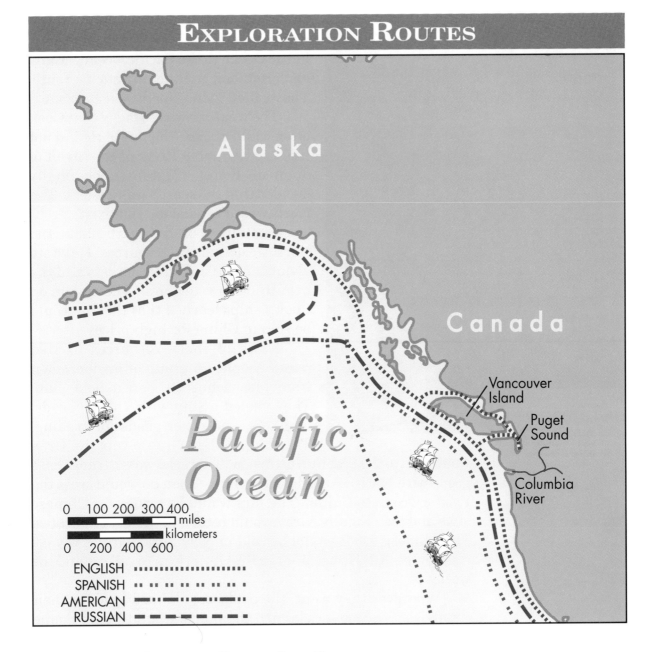

Alaska

Canada

Vancouver Island

Puget Sound

Columbia River

Pacific Ocean

0   100 200 300 400
miles
kilometers
0   200   400   600

ENGLISH ······················
SPANISH ·· · ·· · ·· · ·· ·
AMERICAN ▬·▬·▬·▬·▬·▬
RUSSIAN ▬ ▬ ▬ ▬ ▬ ▬

Other Explorers Come by Sea

Explorers from other countries also sailed along the north Pacific coast. The English explorer George Vancouver made the first maps of Puget Sound. Captain James Cook, another Englishman, made many exploring trips. An American named Robert Gray was the first explorer to sail up the Columbia River.

Captain James Cook was one of the most important English explorers. In 1776, he sailed up the Northwest coast.

George Vancouver.
(Special Collections Division, University of Washington Libraries)

He hoped to find a water route all the way across North America from the Atlantic Ocean to the Pacific Ocean. Many explorers had tried to find such a route. They called it the Northwest Passage.

The weather was so foggy that Cook often could not see the land. He did not find the Columbia River or the Strait of Juan de Fuca. Captain Cook finally decided that the search was useless. The Northwest Passage did not exist.

Captain Cook did learn about the Northwest's natural resources. He wrote about the fish and great forests and the beautiful sea otter furs. The sailors on Cook's ships learned that the furs could be sold in China for high prices.

News of these resources excited many people. A group of businessmen from Massachusetts had a bold plan. They loaded a ship with knives, beads, blankets, and other goods for trading. They hired Robert Gray as captain. Gray would sail to the Pacific Northwest. There, he was to trade these goods with Native Americans for furs. Then he would cross the Pacific Ocean to China. The furs would be traded for Chinese silks and tea. Finally, Gray would return to the United States. The Chinese goods would be sold in New York. Gray's voyage was successful. He became the first American to sail around the world.

Wherever they went, the explorers claimed land for their countries. Vancouver claimed the lands around Puget Sound for England. Robert Gray claimed all the lands around the Columbia River for the United States. For many years, both England and the United States had claims to the land that we now call Washington.

The explorers gave names to the places they saw. Spanish explorers named the San Juan Islands and the nearby waters. George Vancouver chose the names for Puget Sound, Mount Rainier, Whidbey Island, and Hood Canal. Robert Gray named the Columbia River after his ship. Many places were later named for the explorers themselves.

Exploring By Land

The first explorers came to the Pacific Northwest by ship. They stayed along the coast, rarely coming ashore.

Later, other explorers traveled across the region by land. They explored the northwest mountains and river valleys. They learned more about the land and its resources.

The most famous of these overland explorers were Merriwether Lewis and William Clark. They led the first group that traveled across North America to the Pacific Northwest coast.

Lewis and Clark

Lewis and Clark started their trip in 1804. One year earlier, the United States had bought a huge piece of land. It stretched from the Mississippi River to the Rocky Mountains and was called

Robert Gray.
(Special Collections Division, University of Washington Libraries)

the Louisiana Purchase. President Thomas Jefferson asked Lewis and Clark to explore this land and to write about the things they saw.

Lewis and Clark's long journey began in Saint Louis, Missouri. From there, they and a group of men traveled up the Missouri River in a boat. They made other parts of their trip by foot, on horseback, and in simple canoes.

The men spent their first winter in the land of the Mandan tribe. Here they met a young Native American woman named Sacajawea. She traveled with Lewis and Clark across the Rocky Mountains. She helped the explorers get food and horses by trading with her tribe, the Shoshone.

Just before the second winter came, Lewis and Clark reached the Pacific Ocean. They made their winter camp near where Astoria, Oregon, stands today. They called it Fort Clatsop. In spring, the explorers began the long trip home.

Lewis and Clark traded with many Native American tribes along the way. They made notes about the people and their

58

Literature

Lewis and Clark Journal

As the explorers traveled, they kept careful notes. Each day they wrote about where they were and what they saw. These are some notes made by William Clark on his trip down the Columbia River.

"November 5, Tuesday, 1805: Rained all the after part of last night. Rain continues this morning. I slept but very little last night for the noise kept up ... by the swans, geese, white and gray brant ducks, etc. . .

They were extremely numerous and their noise horrid. We met four canoes of Indians from below. . . . The day proved cloudy with rain. . . . We are all wet, cold, and disagreeable. I killed a grouse which was very fat and larger than common.

"November 6, Wednesday, 1805: A cool, wet, rainy morning. We set out early. The Indians of the two lodges we passed today came in their canoes. . . . I purchased two beaver skins for which I gave five small fish hooks. . . . Dried out our bedding and killed the fleas which collected in our blankets. . . .

"November 7, Thursday, 1805: A cloudy, foggy morning. Some rain. . . . Great joy in camp. We are in view of the ocean, this great Pacific Ocean which we have been so anxious to see."

cultures. They wrote about the natural vegetation, the animals, the soil, and other natural resources. Their journey took more than two years.

When they finally returned to Saint Louis, Lewis and Clark were heroes. They had learned much about the new lands, and they helped to give the United States a stronger claim to the Pacific Northwest.

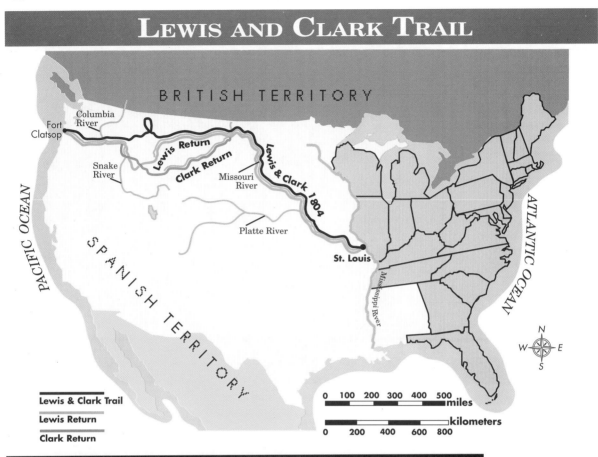

LEWIS AND CLARK TRAIL

BRITISH TERRITORY

Columbia River

Fort Clatsop

Snake River

Lewis Return

Clark Return

Missouri River

Lewis & Clark 1804

Platte River

St. Louis

Mississippi River

PACIFIC OCEAN

SPANISH TERRITORY

ATLANTIC OCEAN

Lewis & Clark Trail
Lewis Return
Clark Return

0 100 200 300 400 500 miles

0 200 400 600 800 kilometers

Lewis and Clark's winter cabins at Fort Clatsop probably looked like this. The men built the cabins and furniture themselves.
(National Park Service)

Lewis and Clark spent their first winter in a Mandan village. This painting shows the explorers in a Mandan home. A black man named York was traveling with Lewis and Clark. The Mandans had never seen a black person, and they were curious about him. York helped the explorers to establish friendly relations with the Native Americans they met. (*York* by C. M. Russell, 1908 watercolor, Montana Historical Society, Helena, MT, gift of the Artist.)

TIME LINES

Time lines like the one shown here are helpful in studying history. They show when important events took place. They help us understand the order in which these events occurred.

A time line is divided into equal parts. In this time line, the space between the big dots equals ten years. The little lines show when an event occurred. The beginning date is at the left. The ending date is at the right.

What time period is shown on this time line? What is the first event shown? What event happened in 1792?

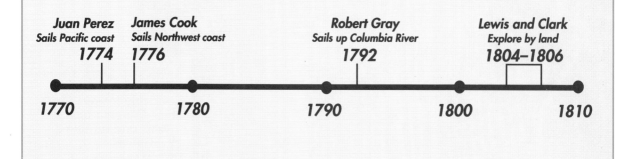

Juan Perez *Sails Pacific coast* 1774
James Cook *Sails Northwest coast* 1776
Robert Gray *Sails up Columbia River* 1792
Lewis and Clark *Explore by land* 1804–1806

1770   1780   1790   1800   1810

The Explorers Come

Word Skills

explorer	Hispanic
claim	ancestor
missionary	natural vegetation

Things to Know

1. Did the first explorers come by land or by sea?

2. List the following explorers on a piece of paper: (a) Bartolome Ferrello, (b) Robert Gray, (c) George Vancouver, (d) James Cook, (e) Lewis and Clark. Beside their names, write the name of the country each represented. Then write one accomplishment of their explorations.

3. Name two reasons why an explorer might choose to make a long, dangerous, and difficult trip.

4. Which two nations claimed land that is now part of Washington State?

5. What was the Louisiana Purchase?

6. Who was Sacajawea?

What Do You Think?

1. Compare the explorers of long ago to the astronauts of today. How are their jobs alike? How are they different?

2. Suppose the Pacific Northwest had remained part of Spain instead of becoming part of the United States. How would your life be different?

3. If you lived long ago, would you have chosen to be an explorer? Why or why not?

River otters, like sea otters, have very soft fur. A large number of the animals were killed for their furs. Today they are protected from hunters.
(The High Desert Museum, Bend, OR)

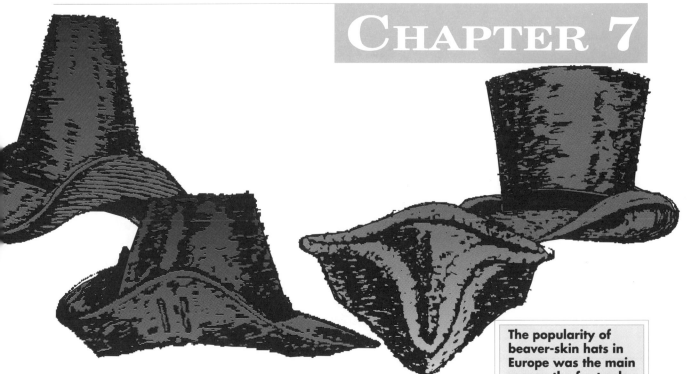

CHAPTER 7

The popularity of beaver-skin hats in Europe was the main reason the fur trade grew.

FUR TRADING DAYS

Think about all the areas of your community. How many wild animals can you think of that live nearby?

Long ago, many more animals roamed the land and waters of the Pacific Northwest. For example, one explorer saw:

bears	raccoons	gray rabbits
wolves	brown minks	squirrels
foxes	martins	mice
deer	beavers	seals
land otters	wild cats	sea otters

Many of these animals had valuable furs. Fur trading became the first big business in the Northwest.

The first traders came by ship. They traded with native hunters for sea otter furs. Then they sailed on, selling furs in Asia, Europe, or big cities of the United States. You read about some of these traders in chapter 6.

64

Literature

Hunting the Sea Otter

Sea otters are fun to watch. But they were not easy to hunt. Captain John Meares was one of the early traders. He observed the Native American hunters and described what he saw.

"Two very small canoes are prepared, in each of which are two skilled hunters. They use bows and arrows and a small harpoon. They proceed among the rocks in search of their prey. A fierce battle often ensues between the otter and the hunters, who are frequently wounded by the claws and teeth of the animal."

The Hudson's Bay Company

Soon, traders came to live in the Pacific Northwest. American and English fur trading companies competed to control the Northwest fur trade. The clear winner of this contest was the Hudson's Bay Company. This powerful English company played an important part in Washington's history.

This is a picture of Fort Vancouver. What activities can you see? For whom do you think the fort was named? (Special Collections Division, University of Washington Libraries)

The Hudson's Bay Company **headquarters** was called Fort Vancouver. It stood where the city of Vancouver, Washington, stands today. The fort itself was a group of buildings with a **stockade,** or tall fence, around them. The stockade was made of strong logs—strong enough for protection in case of an attack.

Inside the fence, there were stores, workshops, and meeting rooms. Outside stood a **sawmill,** a **flour mill,** homes, and other buildings. The officers of the company and their families lived inside the stockade. Other workers lived outside. Many of the traders had Native American wives. There was a small school inside the fort for the few children who lived there.

There also were **vast** farmlands. There were fields of wheat, oats, and barley. There were fruit orchards and vegetable gardens. There were hundreds of farm animals **grazing** nearby.

The people at Fort Vancouver raised more food than they could eat. They sold the rest. The fort was almost like a small city, with all kinds of business going on.

Literature

Life at a Fur Trading Fort

These notes were made by the director of Fort Nisqually. They tell something of the daily life at this fort.

"**December 23, 1833**—Set all hands to work to collect firewood. A few Indians arrived but brought only two beaver to trade. Weather very cold.

"**December 25**—Christmas day. I gave the men eatables and drinkables to make up in some measure for the bad living they have had all year. They enjoyed the feast.

"**February 22, 1834**—Sent five men, and an Indian chief as a protector, to trade with the Clallams. Sent four men on a hunting excursion among the islands of the Sound. The few hands at home employed in airing the furs and goods which I find rather damp.

"**February 27**—The men all employed cutting fence poles. The trade is now very dull. Fine warm weather in the day time but the nights are still cold.

…

Literature

"June 5—From the want of provisions, I had to send two men out hunting deer. Got the road to the Sound completed, and the oxen have brought up all the bark lying on the beach. One man with all the women were employed hoeing earth about the potatoes. Traded 9 beaver skins with the Yakimas. Fine weather.

"August 5—Late in the afternoon, 24 Clallams arrived with a good lot of furs to trade. They received a pipe to smoke and a piece of tobacco for the night.

"August 23—I have this day got into my new dwelling house and I hope in a few days it will be completed. We now have about us three hundred Indians belonging to eight different tribes.

"September 20—The wheat is all in the ground. Gave two young Indian lads a drubbing for riding our horses. A man arrived from Vancouver with letters.

"November 20—This year's returns are:

33 large black bear	1 sea otter
13 small black bear	190 raccoons
1038 large beaver	2 elk
700 rats	(and other animals)"

This park ranger is telling visitors about life at Fort Vancouver. He is standing in a model of the fur trading post.
(National Park Service)

John McLoughlin

The head of Hudson's Bay Company activities in the Northwest was John McLoughlin. The company called him their Chief Factor. But the Native Americans had another name for him: White-headed Eagle.

The Chief Factor had many responsibilities. He ran the business of the Hudson's Bay Company. He directed Fort Vancouver. He decided where the traders would go and how many goods to trade for furs. He made sure that Native Americans were treated fairly. He saw that criminals were punished. He helped people in need. For many years, he was the most powerful person in the Pacific Northwest.

Chief Factor John McLoughlin. The Native Americans called him "White-headed Eagle." Can you see why? (Special Collections Division, University of Washington Libraries)

The Brigades

Each year, McLoughlin sent a large group of traders into the wilderness. The group was known as a brigade. The brigade traveled far into the wilderness, looking for furs. The men trapped and traded as they went.

They were a colorful group. They included Englishmen, Scots, French Canadians, Hawaiians, and Native Americans of many tribes. Some men took their Native American wives and their children along. The brigade leader wore a tall fur hat, a fancy shirt, and a long coat with gold buttons. The members often sang songs as they traveled.

Mountain Men

The most famous fur traders in United States history were the mountain men. These daring, independent trappers generally lived and worked alone. They traveled through the Rocky Mountains without maps or roads to guide them.

Work began in autumn. Every day, the mountain men set their traps. Sometimes they traveled many miles in one day to check them. They cleaned and dried the skins of beavers they caught. The mountain men worked until the heavy snows of winter; then they found shelter. Some had a Native American wife and spent the winter with her tribe.

BEAVERS—NATURE'S ENGINEERS

Beavers are fascinating animals. They have long, sharp teeth for cutting down trees. (Tree bark is their favorite food.) They have webbed feet for swimming. They use their flat tails as building tools.

Few other creatures change the environment as much as beavers. They cut down trees, which they drag to a stream to build dams and create ponds. They some-

This trapper has caught five beavers. Notice their wide, flat tails.
(Special Collections Division, University of Washington Libraries)

times dig canals through the forest. They build complex underground homes. For these reasons, they are sometimes called nature's engineers.

Beavers used to be found in forest streams all over Europe and North America. Then came the fur trade. The beaver's soft inner fur is warm and long-lasting. Hats made of pressed beaver hair were very popular, and beavers were fairly easy to trap. Trappers caught thousands of beavers, and the animal almost became extinct. Today, beavers are plentiful again.

In spring, the trapping started again. Then in summer, when the animals' fur was not as thick, trapping stopped. It was time for the rendezvous. This yearly gathering was held in the valleys of the Rocky Mountains.

The rendezvous was business and party, all in one. The business part was buying and selling. The men sold their furs and used the money to buy supplies. (These might include boots, tobacco, flour, blankets, coffee, gunpowder, and a knife or rifle.) Then came the fun. There were races, feasts, storytelling, and gambling. By the end of the rendezvous, some trappers had spent all they earned.

Some of the mountain men came to the Pacific Northwest. Some even settled here. But it was not easy for them to compete with the powerful Hudson's Bay Company.

Fur Traders Explore the Northwest

The fur trade was important in Washington history for about 60 years, from the 1780s to the 1840s. During that time, trappers and traders learned a lot about the land. They knew the tribes that lived here. They learned about the climate and natural resources. They made some of the first maps of the Pacific Northwest.

Fur Trading Days

Word Skills

compete	sawmill	graze
headquarters	flour mill	brigade
stockade	vast	mountain men
		rendezvous

Things to Know

1. Name the two most important animals in the Northwest fur trade. (Hint: Both are swimmers.)

2. What was the most powerful fur trading company in the Pacific Northwest? Where was this company's headquarters located?

3. Who was the White-headed Eagle? Why was he important in Washington's history?

4. What were the brigades?

5. Who were the mountain men?

6. What two nations competed for the Northwest fur trade?

What Do You Think?

1. Why did the Hudson's Bay Company build their main fort on the Columbia River? Do you think Vancouver was a good location? Why?

2. What kinds of skills do you think it took to be a mountain man? Which of these skills could be learned from Native Americans?

3. Do you think you would like the life of a fur trapper?

4. Do you think the fur traders made it easier for other people to come and live in the Pacific Northwest? Explain.

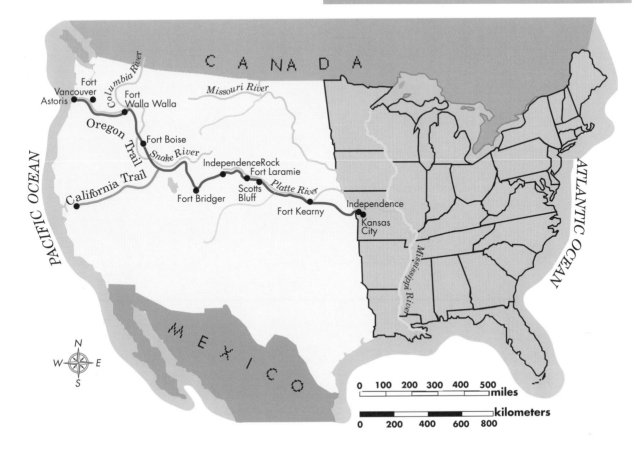

CHAPTER 8

ACROSS THE OREGON TRAIL

During the fur trading years, a few visitors came to the Pacific Northwest. They saw the good farms and businesses of the forts. They saw that the Pacific Northwest was a good place to live.

These visitors wrote and talked about what they had seen. Soon, many people were talking about the good lands of the Pacific Northwest. Some people decided to move here. But how could they travel? There were no roads or trains to the West. The trip by boat was long and difficult.

There was only one thing to do. Travelers would have to make their own trail. People coming to the West from the East followed a route which became known as the Oregon Trail.

For safety, the settlers traveled together in large wagon trains. (Utah State Historical Society)

Wagon Train Days

The Oregon Trail started in Independence, Missouri. It followed the Missouri and Platte rivers. Then it crossed the Rocky Mountains and followed the Columbia River.

Beginning in the 1840s, large groups of settlers traveled across this route. They loaded their possessions into small wooden wagons. One followed another, making a long wagon train. The settlers' horses and cattle walked along behind. The whole group moved very slowly, often just 12 miles a day. (The same distance would take less than 15 minutes by car on today's highways!)

During the daytime, there was work to do. Children gathered firewood as the wagons moved slowly along. Some members of the wagon train rode off on horseback to hunt. If they were lucky, they might shoot a deer or a buffalo to eat. But sometimes food, firewood, and even water were hard to find.

At night, the wagons formed a large circle. In the center of the circle, each family built a fire and cooked a simple dinner.

Study this painting. What does it tell us about being a pioneer? What difficulties do you think pioneers faced when crossing the water? (Utah State Historical Society)

After eating, people often sang songs and shared stories. They slept in the wagons or on the ground. The next morning, after breakfast, they started walking again. This went on day after day, for as long as six months.

The trip across the Oregon Trail was a great and brave adventure. But it was not easy! Every day, it seemed, there were problems and dangers to face.

There were hot and dusty weeks of walking under the burning sun. On other days it rained, and the wagons got stuck in the mud. There were accidents and diseases and no hospitals for the sick. Many travelers, including children, died along the way.

Crossing rivers was always a challenge. Of course, at that time there were no bridges. Sometimes the travelers had to stop and build wooden rafts to carry the wagons. Cows and horses had to swim across, and many animals drowned.

Crossing the mountains was even more difficult. There were trees that had to be chopped down and ditches that had to

be filled. Sometimes there was no grass for the animals to eat. The travelers and their tired animals did the best they could. But it was hard to move the wagons across steep mountain slopes.

Packing Up

Imagine you are leaving your home forever. You are moving to an area that has no stores, no hospitals, no helpful services of any kind. You must pack everything you will need into a wagon barely larger than a modern car. What would you take?

One pioneer recommended that Oregon Trail travelers bring along these things:

flour	lard	grease for wheels	rifle
cornmeal	bacons, wrapped	medicines	axe
sugar	hams, wrapped	extra bedding	shovel
fruit	some vegetables	clothing	rope
molasses	homemade soap	pots and kettles	hammer
butter	salt for animals	water bucket	

Can you think of any other supplies that would be necessary for the trip?

MISSIONARIES

Missionaries were the first American settlers in the Northwest. They came to teach their religion to Native Americans. They started mission farms and schools near the present locations of Salem, Oregon; Walla Walla; Nisqually; and Spokane. As religion teachers, they were not very successful. But the missionaries provided important help to American settlers.

The first wagon train headed west in 1843. With the travelers was one man who already lived in the Northwest. He was a missionary named Marcus Whitman.

Marcus Whitman and his wife, Narcissa settled near where Walla Walla stands today. The model below shows the Whitman's arrival at Fort Vancouver.

Marcus Whitman was a doctor, but he could not cure the diseases that Native Americans caught from the pioneers. Some Native American men grew angry. They killed Marcus, Narcissa and other people at the mission.

(Washington State Travel Development Division)

Literature

A Woman's Point of View

Several women in the wagon trains kept diaries of the trips. Their writing tells about the difficulties faced. These notes were written by Lydia Allen Rudd in 1852.

"June 2 . . . We have had a tedious day. Our road has been sand hills. The sand six inches deep in places and the heat almost intolerable.

"June 12. Passed five graves this morning and a camp where one of their men was dying. . . .

"August 14 . . . Bought a salmon fish of an Indian today weighing 7 or 8 pounds. Gave him an old shirt, some bread, and a sewing needle. . . .

"September 6. We have not been able to leave this miserable place today. I am not as well as yesterday, and no physician to be had. . . .

"September 11 . . . Traveled 14 miles today on the Blue Mountains. Climbed up and down the highest hills that I ever saw a person pass over. Very steep and rocky . . . No water for our stock.

"October 14 . . . I am so anxious to get some place to stop and settle that my patience is not worth much."

A Time of Opportunities

Why did they do it? Why did so many people make this long and difficult trip?

The main reason was land. At the end of the Oregon Trail there was a great deal of good land. For several years, every family that came got a large piece of land for free. Later, when the free land was gone, there were other opportunities. New towns were growing up. These were good places to start businesses.

The West also offered freedom. Some people came across the Oregon Trail to start a new, free life. George Washington Bush was one of them. He was one of the first U.S. citizens to settle the lands of Washington.

GEORGE WASHINGTON BUSH

In 1845, when pioneers began coming to Washington, half the American states still permitted slavery. One dream of many pioneers, both black and white, was to put slavery far behind them.

George Washington Bush was a free African American who hoped he would find a better life in the Pacific Northwest. With his wife, Isabelle, and their sons, he made the long trip across the Oregon Trail. They joined a wagon train led by Mike Simmons.

George W. Bush's life had already been quite full before he started this journey. He had been to school, fought in two wars, and become a successful rancher. Isabelle, a white woman, had been a nurse.

When the Bush family's wagon train arrived in Oregon, they got a sad surprise. Black settlers were not welcome in the Willamette Valley. The pioneers had just voted to keep blacks out.

At that time, the Hudson's Bay Company still controlled the land around Puget Sound. They did not want any Americans to settle there. But George Washington Bush knew that he must try. He finally got permission from the company. He and his family became the first pioneers to settle on land that later became Washington State. A year after Bush arrived, Puget Sound became part of the United States.

George Washington Bush became known as a generous neighbor and a successful farmer. He loaned seeds to the new settlers and helped them start their farms. He got along well with the Native Americans who lived nearby. The place where the Bush family lived is called Bush Prairie, in their honor. It is near the town of Tumwater, which was founded by Mike Simmons.

The American settlers helped give their nation a stronger claim to the land.

The time of the Oregon Trail was an important period in United States history. It was a time of great opportunities. The belief in those opportunities is still an important part of American culture.

Across the Oregon Trail

Word Skills

trail
wagon train
raft

Things to Know

1. What was the Oregon Trail?
2. Name four problems faced by travelers on the Oregon Trail.
3. Name two reasons for making the long and difficult trip across the trail.
4. Who was George Washington Bush?

What Do You Think?

1. If you lived at the time of the Oregon Trail, would you have wanted to join a wagon train? Explain your answer.
2. Why do you think the settlers traveled in large wagon trains? Why didn't they travel alone?
3. Why do you think the Hudson's Bay Company wanted to keep Americans from settling north of the Columbia River?

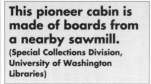

This pioneer cabin is made of boards from a nearby sawmill.
(Special Collections Division, University of Washington Libraries)

Using a spinning wheel, this woman is turning sheep's wool into yarn. This was one of many skills of the pioneers.
(National Park Service)

CHAPTER 9

WASHINGTON PIONEERS

The trip across the Oregon Trail was difficult. Yet it was only the beginning of the hard work for the early settlers, the **pioneers.**

Pioneer families had to build their own homes and furniture. They cut down trees with simple tools. Then they split the logs into rough boards. The first houses they made were small wooden cabins. Often, these had no windows because there was no place to buy glass in the Pacific Northwest.

In fact, there was no place to buy most of the things the pioneers needed. They could not buy stoves, so they built stone fireplaces for heat and cooking. There was no place to buy oil lamps, so the pioneers made candles. They made their own soap, too.

The pioneers had to provide all their own food. This meant clearing trees and rocks from the land so they could raise crops. This was hard work without any of our modern machines. The pioneers also raised cows and made cheese and butter from the milk. They caught fish and killed wild animals such as ducks, deer, and rabbits for meat.

Pioneers made their own shoes and clothing. They raised sheep, cut off the wool, spun it into thread, and wove this into cloth. They got leather for shoes from the animals they killed.

All this work kept the pioneer families very busy. Everyone had to help. Even young children had chores.

For fun, the pioneers liked to tell stories. They also played guessing games and checkers. On special days, they had dances.

MOTHER JOSEPH

Esther Pariseau was a very talented young woman. At age 20, she was already a skilled carpenter. But in 1843, few jobs were open to women. In fact, the only place that would hire her was the Catholic church. She decided to become a nun.

For years, she worked with other nuns in Canada, near her family's home. She mastered many skills including nursing, gardening, candle and soap making, weaving, and sewing. She also learned how to run a business.

Later, she was sent to Vancouver, Washington. She was given a new name—Mother Joseph. (The "mother" is the person in charge of the nuns' activities.)

Mother Joseph must have kept very busy! She started 7 hospitals, 12 schools, and 2 orphanages. She helped build many of the buildings herself. She kept on working until she was almost 80 years old.

Mother Joseph. (Special Collections Division, University of Washington Libraries)

Mother Joseph became one of the most important people in Washington Territory. She is one of two Washington citizens with a statue in the nation's capitol. (The other one is Marcus Whitman.)

Pioneer Schools

One of the first things the settlers wanted was a school for their children. These schools were quite different, of course, from the ones most children attend today. The first schools were very small. Students of all ages shared a single room with one teacher. There were a few books and a few homemade desks in the room. The students walked long distances to school, carrying their lunches in old buckets or boxes.

Often the school year was only three to six months long. The rest of the time, children were needed for work at home.

Pioneer children pose for a picture on a large tree stump. (Special Collections Division, University of Washington Libraries)

84

Literature

A Pioneer Childhood

"I was brought to Washington Territory by my parents in 1877. We came by train to San Francisco and by boat to Neah Bay. My father cooked in the Indian school. He was fascinated with this country. He thought it was the garden spot of the world.

"He built a log house for the family, and I grew up there. In that log house, I listened to wolves howling. They sometimes caught our sheep. The cougar's cry sounded like a lost child. The elk whistled and the bears seemed to bark.

"There was no church, so father and mother held Sunday school in our house. Father established a post office, and my brother carried the mail on his back from Cape Flattery to Quilleute.

"I was a good shot and practiced with the boys. Once I competed with father and beat him at target shooting.

"We rode horseback over trails, or walked, or rode in Indian canoes on the ocean. Once when I was sick, I was hauled out over the trail on a sled 40 miles across the mountains to Clallam.

"On Christmas, we always had a tree. We made all our presents. We had a fine Christmas dinner with all kinds of meat, ducks, geese, chickens, plenty of eggs, and lots of cream, with cakes and strawberry pie. Then in the evening we had dancing in one of the larger houses. My brother played the violin."

(Told by Jennie S. Tyler, in the Works Progress Administration book *Told by the Pioneers*, 1939, pp. 37–39)

Who Owned the Northwest?

Before the pioneers arrived, the Pacific Northwest was Indian land. A few fur traders were the only other residents. The Hudson's Bay Company, owned by the English, controlled the region's trade.

Then thousands of American settlers began arriving each year. These settlers hoped the Pacific Northwest would soon become part of the United States. The earlier residents, the English and the Native Americans, did not want to give up their land. Somehow, this conflict would have to be resolved.

An Agreement Between England and the United States

The first Northwest pioneers settled on the rich farmland of the Willamette Valley of Oregon. Soon there were more American settlers than fur traders living there. It was clear that this land would become part of the United States. But the Hudson's Bay Company still controlled the area north of the Columbia River. England still had a strong claim to Puget Sound.

A WAR OVER PIGS AND POTATOES?

The agreement between England and the United States left one thing unclear. Who owned the San Juan Islands? (This is a group of small islands located a little south of the U.S.–Canada border at the north end of Puget Sound.) Both countries thought the islands should be theirs. American and English settlers there grew angry and suspicious of each other.

One day, an Englishman's pig escaped into a farm owned by an American. The pig ate some of the farmer's potatoes. The farmer complained, "Keep your pig on your own land!" The man refused. The American farmer shot the pig.

The anger between English and American settlers grew stronger. Both nations sent troops to the islands. The countries seemed close to war.

But instead of fighting, they asked William I, the ruler of Germany, to decide. William listened to the arguments of both sides. He decided that the U.S. claim to the San Juan Islands was stronger. Ever since then, the San Juans have been part of Washington.

However, the United States also wanted Puget Sound and the lands around it. There was talk of war to decide which country would get the land, but neither country really wanted to fight. Finally, in 1846, the two nations signed an agreement.

England would keep Vancouver Island and the land north of 49 degrees north latitude. These lands later became part of Canada.

The United States would keep the land to the south. This is the region we now call the Pacific Northwest.

As more settlers arrived, new towns grew up. This is a view of Seattle in pioneer times. (Special Collections Division, University of Washington Libraries)

Native Americans Respond to New Settlers

Most Native Americans had been friendly to the fur traders. But the pioneers brought many problems. Pioneer settlers took too much land. They killed the fish and animals that the tribes depended on for food. The newcomers also brought new diseases, such as measles, and many Native Americans died.

Some Native Americans decided to fight. Some attacked wagon trains that crossed their land. Some went to war to protect their way of life.

Other tribes made a different decision. They saw that more settlers were coming each year. "We will soon be outnumbered," they said. "It is better to make peace with the newcomers."

Most of the tribes signed agreements, called treaties, with the U.S. government. The tribes agreed to sell most of their land and move to certain areas set aside for them. These protected lands are called reservations. In return, the government promised that the tribes could continue to fish and hunt for food and live in peace.

NEW FOODS, NEW TASTES

Fur traders and pioneers brought new foods to the Northwest. Native people tried them, but did not always like them. This story was told by William Mason, a coastal Indian.

"I first tasted potatoes, bread, vegetables and other white man's food when ten years of age. Indian food is mostly fish, whale meat, sea lion, elk, deer, and bear. These things we killed. . . . Cornflakes and fruit are the only food of the white man I like." (*Told by the Pioneers*, WPA, p. 160)

Chief Sealth and Chief Joseph: Two Leaders Make Different Choices

Chief Sealth was a Suquamish Indian. The city of Seattle was named after him. Like most of the coastal Indian leaders, Sealth decided to sign a treaty. He said:

"The settlers are many. They are like the grass that covers vast prairies. My people are few as the trees on a storm-swept plain. You say you will buy our lands and give us enough to live on comfortably. We will accept your offer. But to us the land of our ancestors will always be special. Every hillside, every plain and forest is filled with their spirits. The white man will never be alone. Our spirits will always be here."

Chief Joseph was a leader of the Nez Perce, a plateau tribe. Life on the plateau was harder than on the coast. It was harder to find food. Without their vast hunting lands, the Nez Perce might not survive. Knowing this, many Nez Perce wanted to fight. They won several battles against the U.S. Army. With Chief Joseph leading them, they tried to escape into Canada. But just before the Nez Perce reached the border, the army

Chief Joseph led the Nez Perce. (Special Collections Division, University of Washington Libraries)

Chief Sealth, after whom Seattle was named. (Special Collections Division, University of Washington Libraries)

attacked. Many members of the tribe were killed and Joseph surrendered. "My heart is sick and sad," he said. "From where the sun now stands, I will fight no more forever."

Washington Pioneers

Word Skills

pioneer	conflict
territory	treaty
resident	reservation

Things to Know

1. Name at least five things the pioneers had to make for themselves.

2. How were pioneer children's lives different from your own? Give at least three examples.

3. What agreement did the United States and England make in 1846?

4. What agreements did Native Americans make in the treaties? What promises did the government make?

What Do You Think?

1. Pretend you are a Native American leader when pioneers started coming in large numbers. How would you recommend your tribe act toward settlers? Make up a speech to give your opinion.

2. Imagine that you lived in pioneer times. What things would be fun or pleasing about your life? What things would be difficult or unpleasant?

Train station in Garfield, eastern Washington. (Special Collections Division, University of Washington Libraries)

CHAPTER 10

This was the first train to go across the United States to Puget Sound. Why were railroads so important to Puget Sound cities? (Special Collections Division, University of Washington Libraries)

RAILROADS BRING GROWTH AND CHANGE

The year was 1848. Oregon Territory had just been created. This was the first official government in the Pacific Northwest.

But the most exciting event of that year took place far to the south. Gold was discovered in California! The next year, thousands of people hurried to California hoping to find gold and "strike it rich." The gold rush had begun.

California was booming. The population was growing fast. More and more people wanted to go west, but travel was difficult. It was time to build a railroad.

The first cross-country railroad was completed in 1869. Americans could now travel by train from the Atlantic coast to San Francisco.

Settlers benefited from the California gold rush in several ways. Logs and lumber were needed to build docks and buildings for the growing city of San Francisco. Much of the wood came from Washington forests. Coal was another Washington product that was needed in California. Soon, many ships were traveling between San Francisco and the new towns around Puget Sound.

COAL MINING

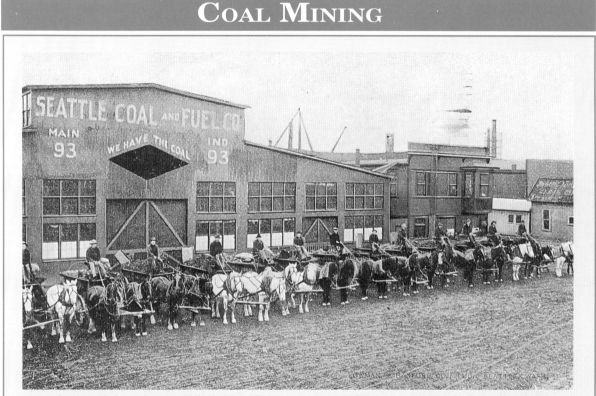

In early Seattle, coal was delivered to homes in horse-drawn wagons. A lot of people used to burn coal to heat their houses. How do you heat your home today? (Special Collections Division, University of Washington Libraries)

Gold and silver were not the only important minerals in the Pacific Northwest. Coal was also important. It was found in the Lowlands and the Cascade Mountains.

Many people found work in Washington's **coal** mines. Some of the early **miners** were Chinese. Others came from England or Wales. The first large group of African Americans in Washington came here to dig coal in these mines. Even children found work sorting the pieces of coal.

Thanks to the California railroad, there was an easier way to get to the Northwest. Settlers could now take the train to San Francisco and then take a ship to Puget Sound.

This was much easier than the trip across the Oregon Trail.

But the northwest settlers wanted their own railroad. A railroad would bring many new settlers to the region. It would help the young Washington cities to grow. It would bring eastern products, such as stoves, glass, and cotton cloth.

Finally, the U.S. government gave permission for a railroad to be built. The first northwest railroad was called the Northern Pacific. The tracks ran from Minnesota to Portland and then north to Tacoma.

The other cities on Puget Sound were disappointed by the choice of Tacoma. They all wanted a railroad. The citizens of Seattle were especially angry. They decided to build their own railroad. But they soon found that this was very hard work. They gave up after building only a small part. However, ten years later they got their wish. A new railroad was finally completed to Seattle. It was called the Great Northern.

JAMES J. HILL

As a boy growing up in Canada, Jim Hill wanted to be a doctor. But an accident left him blind in one eye. He went to work in a store when he was 14 years old. Later he left home for Minnesota and went to work on a steamboat. Soon, he owned his own shipping business.

Then he began buying and building railroads. He went on to run the Great Northern Railroad Company.

James Hill helped bring new settlers to the Northwest. He helped Washington's businesses grow. He became an important person in our state's history.

James J. Hill gives a speech. (Special Collections Division, University of Washington)

Workers from Many Nations

The job of building a railroad was not easy. In those days, people had no big machines to help them move dirt or build bridges. Everything had to be done by hand.

Thousands and thousands of workers helped build the great railroads of the West. The workers came from Europe and Asia and many parts of the United States. They worked ten hours a day in the burning heat of summer and freezing cold of winter. The work was hard, and it was often dangerous.

There were many jobs to be done. One group of workers used picks, shovels, and plows to make a flat and level path. They built bridges over rivers and blasted tunnels through the mountains. The next group laid the ties. These were heavy bars of wood, eight feet long. Then other workers laid iron rails across the ties. Finally, the rails were attached to the ties with long, thick nails, called spikes. Imagine pounding spikes with heavy hammers for ten hours! For all this hard work, the men earned $1.75 a day.

One of the largest groups of railroad workers came from China. Many people in China were very poor. News of the California gold discovery caused much excitement. "There's a mountain of gold in America!" people said. Thousands of Chinese decided to join the gold rush. They hoped to earn some money and then return to their families in China.

However, Chinese workers were met with **prejudice** in the United States. The good gold mining areas were closed to them. So were other good jobs. The Chinese men had to find other ways to earn a living. Some of them started small businesses, such as restaurants or laundries. Many more went to work for the railroads. After laying the tracks to California, many Chinese helped build the railroads in Washington.

CHIN GEE HEE

Chin Gee Hee was probably the best-known Chinese settler in Washington Territory. He started a laundry business in Port Gamble and later went to work for the railroad. After a while, he was in charge of hiring workers to build the roads. He settled in Seattle and became a well-known businessman. He returned to China as a rich man.

Chin Gee Hee owned a store like this in Seattle.
(Special Collections Division, University of Washington Libraries)

EARLY HOTELS

Spokane was a railroad center and soon had several elegant hotels for travelers. But the first hotel in the city was simple indeed! This is how one pioneer described it:

"Bear skins and buffalo hides were laid on the floor to serve as beds. A ladder offered the only means of reaching the second floor, and there were no maids. . . . The guests were mostly cowboys and miners. They enjoyed washing and bathing in clear cold water from a half barrel in which floated several bars of soap."

Literature

A Japanese Boy and the Railroad

My work was to cut down trees or to construct the railroads, digging and filling land in the mountains. It was quite hard work. I was only a boy of a little more than 15, having just graduated from grade school. Since I had never done hard physical labor, when I worked 10 or 12 hours a day, the next morning I couldn't open my hands. For two or three months, I dipped them in hot water for a while in order to stretch the fingers back to normal and sometimes I secretly cried. My pay was $1.75 for 10 hours. I had good reason to work my hardest, gritting my teeth, for when I left Japan, I had promised my mother, whose health was not good, "I'll surely come back to Japan in a year." (From *Issei*, by Kazuo Ito Japanese Community Service, Seattle, 1973)

Railroads Bring Growth and Change

Word Skills

gold rush   miner

population   spike

coal   prejudice

Things to Know

1. What happened in California in 1848?

2. Why did Washington need railroads?

3. Name the first two cross-country railroads that reached Puget Sound. In which city did each railroad end?

4. Name at least one person or group who helped build the northwest railroads. What contribution did they make?

What Do You Think?

1. Suppose you lived in the eastern United States in 1848. Would you have joined the gold rush? How would you have traveled to California? What would you have taken with you?

2. Suppose that it is before the railroads were built. Most of Western Washington is still covered with forest. Where could the pioneers sell this lumber? How could they transport it?

3. Imagine you are a Washington pioneer. What changes would the railroads bring to your life? List as many things as you can think of.

Statehood day, November 11, 1889. The old state capitol was decorated for the occasion. (Special Collections Division, University of Washington Libraries)

CHAPTER 11

WASHINGTON BECOMES A STATE

When Oregon Territory was first created, it was very large. It included the present states of Washington, Oregon, and Idaho. It also included parts of present-day Montana and Wyoming.

In those days, most American settlers in the territory lived near the Willamette River. The center of **territorial government** was located in the Willamette River Valley.

Soon, the northern and eastern parts of the territory began to grow. Pioneers started cities around Puget Sound. Mining towns grew up in the Rocky Mountains.

It was hard to travel from these new towns and cities to the Willamette River. There were few roads, and the trip took a long time. The northern and eastern settlers felt cut off from the territory's government.

The Puget Sound settlers got together. They wrote letters to the leaders of the U.S. government. They asked that Oregon Territory be divided into parts.

This happened in 1853. The area that is today known as the state of Oregon then became Oregon Territory. The rest of the Pacific Northwest was called Washington Territory. It had a separate government, centered in Olympia.

Statehood!

Washington's territorial government set up schools and other services. It helped solve problems of the pioneers. But the pioneers believed a state government would be even better.

In a state, government leaders are chosen by people who live there. In a territory, the top government leaders are chosen by the U.S. president. In a territory, settlers did not have so much control over their government and their laws.

To become a state, a few things had to happen. First, the population had to grow large enough. Then, the people of the territory had to vote to become a state. (In those days, only white men over age 21 could vote.) Finally, the U.S. government had to approve Washington for statehood.

The people of Washington Territory had to wait a long time. The population did not grow large enough for statehood until the railroads came. Washington finally became a state in 1889. It was the 42nd state of the nation.

People of Many Nations

If you had lived in Europe in the middle to late 1800s, you would probably have heard many stories about America. You might have had friends or family members who had moved to the United States.

There were many reasons to make the long trip. Europe was crowded. There were not enough jobs. The United States was a place of opportunity. There was plenty of land for farming, and there were many jobs. There were opportunities to start new businesses. And there was freedom.

Millions of Europeans decided to move to the United States. They became immigrants (people who leave their homeland to move to a new place). Many thousands of immigrants came to Washington State on the railroads. The largest group was from Scandinavia, or the countries of Sweden, Norway, and Denmark. The land around Puget Sound reminded the Scandinavian families of home. Many of them settled in the fishing town of Ballard, which later became part of Seattle.

The next largest group were English-speaking people from England, Scotland, Ireland, and Wales. Many of them worked in Washington mines and cities. They named several Washington towns. For example, Aberdeen is named for a city in Scotland. Conway is a name from Wales.

Germans were the third largest group of Europeans to arrive. Among this group was William Bremer, for whom Bremerton was named. Seattle businessman Henry Yesler was another well-known German American. He owned a lumber business and shipping dock and was one of early Seattle's leading citizens. Many Germans settled in Eastern Washington and became farmers.

Jewish Americans who have contributed to Washington history include Edward Saloman, a governor of Washington Territory.

Other Europeans in Washington included families from Russia, Italy, France, Greece, Yugoslavia, and other nations. They included farmers, fishers, miners, and business owners. They helped build communities around Washington State.

Japanese Americans helped build the oyster farming business of the Pacific Northwest. These are some early oyster farmers. (Special Collections Division, University of Washington Libraries)

Literature

Japanese Workers in Washington

One growing group of newcomers did not come to Washington by train. They came across the Pacific Ocean by ship from Japan. Most of them were young, unmarried men. They planned to work a while, save money, and then go back to Japan. These Japanese men had many of the same jobs and many of the same problems as the Chinese workers. They found prejudice, poor jobs, and low pay. This is the experience of one Japanese worker:

"Since bread was expensive, and we couldn't afford the same food as whites, we ate dumpling soup for breakfast and supper. ... We worked 10 hours a day and made $1.15. ... White workers got $1.45 a day. Two or three months of the winter we were out of a job. ... We took turns cooking every day.

"For three years and a half, I worked this way and sent the money—nearly 1,000 Yen—to my father in Okayama. He bought about a five-acre field and suddenly became a rich man in the village." (From *Issei*, by Kazuo Ito, Japanese Community Service, Seattle, 1973, p. 395)

Making a New Home

Making a new home in the United States was full of challenges. Most of the immigrants did not speak English. They had little money and little knowledge of American life. There was a lot to learn!

People of the same language and culture helped each other. They set up organizations to provide services such as language classes and help for the sick. Often the groups built churches, temples, or community halls. These served as important gathering places. Many such buildings and organizations can be found in Washington today.

Literature

Coming to the United States

The trip to the United States was not easy. This story was told by a boy who left his village in Italy to travel to the United States with his family.

"We had no idea what was in store for us. We were loaded onto a neighbor's mule and taken to the train. In Genoa, we went aboard the ancient [ship]. . . . We had left the Old Country. We were moving slowly toward a mysterious New World. . . .

"I remember that it was a rough passage. We were packed in filthy bunks like herring in a barrel. All our belongings were crowded there with us—even the tin dishes in which we ate the awful food we were served." (From *Immigrant's Return*, by Angelo Pellegrini, New York: MacMillan, 1951)

Many immigrants settled in Washington, bringing their culture and customs with them. Folk dance groups like this one help keep those customs alive today. (University of Washington *Daily*)

After a time, the immigrants learned English. They became Americans. But they did not want to forget the good things about their old homelands. They found ways to share their language, cooking, religion, and art with families and friends.

The United States on the Move

Of course, many people who came to Washington were already Americans. They came here on the railroads from other parts of the United States. They came for farmland, good jobs, and a pleasant place to live.

Among them were the state's first large group of African Americans. They came to work in the mines in the Cascade Mountains. Later, many of them settled in the cities. Some helped build the railroads. Others worked on the ships that sailed up and down the West Coast. A few started small businesses, such as barber shops.

In Washington, as in the rest of the United States, African Americans found prejudice. They were not allowed to live in some areas. They were kept out of most jobs and were forced to sit in separate seating areas in theaters. African Americans often could not get service in restaurants or hotels.

Still, African Americans had more opportunities in Washington than in many states. Many had good homes in the cities. Some owned farms. Like other groups of newcomers, they helped each other. They played a part in building Washington's communities.

The men and women who built Washington cities came from many lands and cultures. Horace Cayton was a Seattle newspaper publisher. (Special Collection Davision, University of Washington Libraries)

Thea Foss was a Norwegian American who started the largest tugboat company on Puget Sound. (Special Collections Division, University of Washington Libraries)

MAY HUTTON

May Arkwright was living in Ohio when she heard about the gold and silver discoveries in the Northwest. She was one of thousands of people who hurried to the northwest mines.

Life in the mining areas was rough and often wild, but May was not afraid. She knew what she wanted. She would open a restaurant and make money selling food to the miners. Someday, maybe, she would be rich.

May started her business and later married one of her customers. He was a railroad worker named Al Hutton. Together with some other people, the Huttons bought a mine. May kept her restaurant, and Al kept working for the railroad. But they worked in the mine whenever they could. So did the other owners. They all kept on digging for four years. Then one day they found silver. All the owners became millionaires.

May Arkwright Hutton said, "The Lord gave me money to serve!" She worked to make life better for people in the Pacific Northwest. The Huttons settled in Spokane and became two of that city's leading citizens.

This photo shows the Huttons' mine and all its owners. May is sitting near the center of the group. Al is standing on the right. What important mineral did they find in this mine? (See page 103.) (University of Idaho)

Alexander Pantages was a Greek American who started theaters in Puget Sound cities and around the country. (Special Collections Division, University of Washington Libraries)

Bertha Landes was elected mayor of Seattle in 1924. She was the first woman mayor of a large U.S. city.
(Historical Society of Seattle and King County)

FIRE!

In pioneer days, all buildings were made of wood. Washington sawmills provided the lumber, and settlers were proud of their new homes and stores.

But there was a problem. Wooden buildings burn easily. In 1889, the year of statehood, both Seattle and Spokane had terrible fires. Large areas of the cities were destroyed.

Citizens were not discouraged, though. They ran their businesses out of tents until new brick buildings were put up.

Washington Becomes a State

Word Skills

territorial government
services
immigrant

Things to Know

1. What present-day states were part of Oregon Territory?
2. When did Washington become a territory?
3. When did Washington become a state?

What Do You Think?

1. Is it easier to feel prejudice toward someone who does not speak your language than toward someone who does? Why or why not? What about someone who looks and dresses differently?

2. If you had to leave the United States and become an immigrant, what things would you miss?

3. If you made a fortune suddenly, as May and Al Hutton did, how would you spend your money?

108

EDISON PHONOGRAPH

Are the Best

OWN ONE:
THE GEM, $10.00; THE STANDARD, $20.00;
THE HOME, $30.00.

EDISON RECORDS
Smooth, Sweet and Natural

As Edison's Jobbers we will deliver these Phonographs to you at the ist price. We carry 10,000 Records in stock at all times. Send for catalogues. Correspondence solicited.

THE DENVER DRY GOODS CO.,
DENVER, COLO.

National Phonograph Company
Orange, New Jersey.

Ads in catalogs let people know about new inventions that could make their lives better. These phonographs were the early version of our modern-day stereo turntable.
(*Outdoor Life*, 1905)

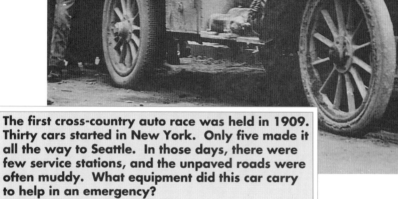

The first cross-country auto race was held in 1909. Thirty cars started in New York. Only five made it all the way to Seattle. In those days, there were few service stations, and the unpaved roads were often muddy. What equipment did this car carry to help in an emergency?
(Historical Society of Seattle & King County)

CHAPTER 12

WASHINGTON STATE: THE FIRST 50 YEARS

In 1890, Washington citizens were proud of their new state. They were proud, too, of the new technology that was changing the way people lived.

Many new inventions were making life easier. Telephones, elevators, and electric streetcars were all examples. The first phone in Yakima was in the Yakima Hotel. It was only turned on for part of the day. Spokane was one of the first western cities with electric streetlights.

The first streetcars were pulled by horses. Once in a while, the horses became frightened and ran away with the car! Electric streetcars came soon afterward to Tacoma, Seattle, Yakima, and other Washington cities.

Then came the automobile. Some people were excited about this new machine. Other people disapproved. They thought that 20 miles an hour was just too fast to go! There were problems, of course. The first cars did not always run very well. There were no traffic lights or stop signs, which often made driving confusing.

TWO WASHINGTON PHOTOGRAPHERS

Photography was still a fairly new technology at the turn of the century. Few people owned cameras. However, two early Washington photographers became quite famous. They were Edward Curtis and Imogen Cunningham.

Edward Curtis came to Seattle in 1888. He set up a small shop where people could come and have their pictures taken. But Edward Curtis had a dream. He wanted to photograph Native Americans.

Native cultures were changing fast. Curtis gave up his shop and began traveling. For 30 years, he visited tribes around the country. He talked with people, took pictures, and wrote about what he learned. His photographs are an important historical record and an important work of art. You can see a photograph by Curtis on page 47.

Imogen Cunningham bought her first camera when she was a teenager. She worked for a while in Edward Curtis's shop. Then she studied photography in Europe. She invented a new way to make photographic paper. And she took wonderful photos! She kept working until she was over 90 years old.

In 1880, only 350 people lived in Spokane. Thirty years later, the population was 100,000. The growth of businesses made this possible. (Special Collections Division, University of Washington Libraries)

View of historic Yakima. Like all of Washington's cities, Yakima grew around the early 1900s. (Special Collections Division, University of Washington Libraries)

City Growth

The young Washington cities were growing fast. Blocks of tall, new brick buildings filled the downtown areas. Neighborhoods grew up around the city center. Paved streets replaced the old dirt roads. Stores were full of products that the pioneers had never even imagined.

The cities were growing, but they were still surrounded by wilderness. There is an interesting story in a magazine article from 1894. The writer took a 12-mile train ride from Tacoma to Steilacoom. The route led through dense forest.

"I noticed a man on the front platform of the car. He carried a gun that he now and then pointed. . . . Finally he fired. Immediately, the train was stopped, and the hunter picked up a rabbit he had just killed."

Seattle Takes the Lead

Seattle was already the state's largest city. Several things helped the city grow. One interesting example was the Klondike gold rush.

Gold had been discovered along the Klondike River in Alaska. As the news spread, thousands of people headed for Alaska, hoping to strike it rich. A large number bought their supplies and boarded ships in Seattle. Seattle's businesses grew quickly and so did its population.

This ship arrived in Seattle with a million dollars worth of Alaska gold.
(Special Collections Division, University of Washington Libraries)

This is how an early textbook for Seattle schoolchildren described the time:

"The gold rush began pouring millions of dollars into the city. Outfitting stores, specializing in the needs of the gold seekers, centered the trade here. Working day and night, they struggled to keep up with their orders. The sidewalks were piled high with goods awaiting shipment to the north." (J. Willis Sayre, *This City of Ours,* Seattle School District #1, 1936)

Washington Agriculture

There was growth in the farming areas, too. New crops were introduced. The first irrigation systems were built in Eastern Washington. Apples and other fruits were some of the crops raised on irrigated lands.

People of many lands and cultures helped develop Washington agriculture. Italian farmers near Walla Walla raised vegetables, including the big, sweet onions that are now famous. Japanese farmers developed the state's strawberry crop. Dutch settlers planted tulips and daffodils in the Skagit River Valley. Today, you can see miles of colorful flowers in this valley each spring.

Japanese farm workers on a western Washington strawberry farm. (Special Collections Division, University of Washington Libraries)

Even with new machines, farming was hard work. Many people were needed to tend and harvest the crops. This low-paying work was often done by newcomers to the United States.

Chinese immigrants were some of the first farm workers. Some people became afraid that Chinese men were taking too many jobs. The government passed a law saying that the Chinese were no longer allowed to come to this country.

They were replaced by workers from Japan. Later, Japanese people were also **excluded.** The next group of farm workers came from the Philippines. They, too, were later kept from coming to the United States.

CARLOS BULOSAN, FILIPINO POET

The Philippines is an island nation that was ruled for many years by the United States. Filipinos grew up hearing stories about the United States. Many young Filipinos came to the United States in search of a better life. But like other Asian immigrants, they found prejudice.

One of these young men was Carlos Bulosan. He wrote about his experiences in a book called *America Is in the Heart.* This is part of what he said:

"America is not a land of one race or one class of men. We are all Americans that have toiled and suffered . . . from the first Indian . . . to the last Filipino pea pickers . . . We are America!"

Carlos Bulosan
(Special Collections
Division, University of
Washington Libraries)

The logging camps were crowded and uncomfortable. Loggers joined together in unions to improve their working conditions. (Special Collections Division, University of Washington Libraries)

Labor Unions

Foreign workers were not the only group with problems. In those days, it was common to work ten or twelve hours a day, six days a week. Even young children might work this long. Working conditions were often bad. For example, loggers lived in dirty, crowded cabins with little heat and poor food. Mines and sawmills were unsafe, and many workers were killed or injured. The pay was very low. People worked all day and were still very poor.

The solution to these problems is clear, some people said. Workers must join together to insist on improvements.

Many workers did come together to form **labor unions.** Washington State, and Seattle especially, had some of the largest, strongest labor unions in the country. With the help of these unions, Washington workers were able to win higher wages, shorter work days, and safer jobs.

Sometimes union members stopped working, refusing to go back until they won these improvements. This is called going on **strike.** Once, nearly all the workers in Seattle went on strike for five days. It was one of the only **general strikes** in the nation's history.

115

Washington women worked hard to win the right to vote.
(Special Collections Division, University of Washington Libraries; Asahel Curtis)

Washington Women Win the Right to Vote

The early 1900s were a time of change. A lot of people were working for better lives. As a result, several important laws were passed. Some of these laws protected workers. Another law gave Washington women the right to vote.

In those days, Wyoming was the only state where women could vote. All over the United States, women were organizing to win this important right. Washington was one of the first places they were successful. Washington women became voters in state elections in 1910. Ten years later, all U.S. women won voting rights. They could take part in local, state, and national elections.

The Great Depression

The 1920s were a time of growth for American businesses. For a while, it seemed the growth would go on forever. Then came disaster! In 1929, the nation entered the Great Depression.

During the Great Depression, these simple shacks were home to many men in Seattle. The men called the area Hooverville, after President Herbert Hoover. He was president when the depression began. (Special Collections Division, University of Washington Libraries; James P. Lee)

A depression is a time when many companies lose business. A lot of people lose their jobs. Because there is no work, people have little money to spend.

During the Great Depression, a very large number of Americans were out of work. Many people had no place to live. Long lines of people waited each day for a bowl of soup to eat. It was the worst depression in our nation's history.

At the worst times, factories closed and thousands of people lost their jobs. People could not pay for food or clothing. They could not pay the rent. Stores went out of business. It worked like a circle.

The New Deal

In 1932, the voters elected a new president, Franklin Delano Roosevelt. He had a plan to help end the depression. He called it the New Deal. One part of the plan was to create jobs. Many people were hired for new building projects.

In Washington State, the largest New Deal projects were dams. The Grand Coulee and Bonneville dams were both built during this time. Other workers built parks, trails, buildings, and roads around the state.

Even with these projects, the depression went on. It lasted for more than ten years.

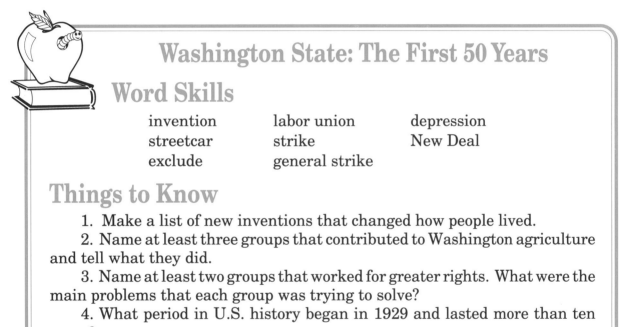

Washington State: The First 50 Years

Word Skills

invention	labor union	depression
streetcar	strike	New Deal
exclude	general strike	

Things to Know

1. Make a list of new inventions that changed how people lived.

2. Name at least three groups that contributed to Washington agriculture and tell what they did.

3. Name at least two groups that worked for greater rights. What were the main problems that each group was trying to solve?

4. What period in U.S. history began in 1929 and lasted more than ten years?

What Do You Think?

1. What inventions were needed before very tall buildings could be built? Think of at least one example and tell why it was important.

2. Is it important for all Americans to have the right to vote? Why? Are there any groups that should not be allowed to vote? (For example, at what age do you think people should be able to vote?)

3. The Klondike gold rush brought lots of business to Seattle and helped the city grow. What people or events have helped your community grow? Why was this important? (You can pick an event from recent times or from community history.)

The United States printed posters to support the World Wars. This one is from World War One, which took place from 1914 to 1918. (Special Collections Division, University of Washington Libraries)

CHAPTER 13

THE MODERN PERIOD

In the last several chapters, you have learned about the early days of Washington history. This chapter is about more recent times. It tells about events your parents or grandparents may remember.

Many people say that the modern period of history began with World War II. This terrible war brought changes in the lives of people around the world.

What Was World War II?

In the 1930s three powerful nations began to make war against their neighbors. These nations, called the **Axis powers,** were Germany, Italy, and Japan. Their large armies invaded one country after another. By 1941, most of Europe, North Africa, and East Asia were under Axis control.

On December 7, 1941, Japan bombed the U.S. navy base at Pearl Harbor, Hawaii. The United States entered the war.

Sixteen million Americans fought in World War II. They joined the troops from England, Canada, France, the Philippines, the Soviet Union, and other nations to fight against the Axis powers. These nations were known as the **Allies.**

In 1945, the United States and its allies were successful. First, Germany and Italy were defeated, and the war ended in Europe. In August 1945, the United States dropped two **atomic bombs** on Japan. The Japanese government surrendered two days afterward. World War II was over.

Washington State During the War

Washington citizens contributed to the war effort in many ways. Thousands of young men and women joined the armed forces. The army, navy, and air force bases in our state were very busy.

Washington farms and factories were busy, too. They produced food, airplanes, ships, trucks, aluminum, and other

A navy ship in Washington during World War II.
(Historical Society of Seattle & King County)

products needed for the war. Workers at Hanford helped make the atomic bombs that were dropped on Japan.

With so many men away in the armed forces, Washington businesses needed to find new workers. During the war years, many women went to work in factories for the first time. Thousands more workers came to Washington from other parts of the country. Among them were many African Americans. They came from southern states and played an important role in Washington's war effort.

Most of the new jobs were in the cities. But workers were also needed on the farms, especially at harvest time. The United States created a special program to bring farm workers from Mexico. These Mexican workers came to Washington each year to harvest crops. They were important to Washington agriculture, both during and after the war.

Even schoolchildren participated in the war effort. They helped collect aluminum for recycling. They made warm scarves and mittens for our soldiers. Many older children worked part-time.

After the War

World War II was the biggest war in history. When it ended, the United States was stronger than ever. There were lots of new jobs, and Americans were earning more money than ever before.

Like other states, Washington grew steadily. New factories were started. There were new farms and new farm products, such as sugar beets and grapes. The population kept growing, too.

The cities grew especially fast. New communities, called suburbs, grew up around the city centers. Families depended more on cars to get to work and go shopping. Many new roads were built.

Changes in transportation and communication helped link Washington cities with the rest of the world. The state's first television station was started in 1949. The Seattle-Tacoma airport opened that same year. Work on the state's freeways began about ten years later. People could now travel more easily and see TV programs from other places. Washington no longer seemed so far away from the rest of the nation.

JAPANESE AMERICANS AND WORLD WAR II

Life was hard for the first Japanese in Washington State. Still, some of the young men decided to stay here. They wrote to their families in Japan. The families arranged for the men to be married. They chose a young woman and sent her picture to the man in the United States. When the boat arrived from Japan, the man used the picture to find his bride.

By World War II, some of these families had lived here for more than 40 years. Most were American citizens.

Then came Pearl Harbor. Many Americans were afraid. They feared that Japan might try to attack the west coast states. They feared that Japanese Americans might help Japan.

In 1942, the U.S. government gave an order. All people of Japanese ancestry must leave the West Coast. They would live in special **internment** camps until the war was over.

The camps were located in the desert and were surrounded by wire fences. Families lived in rows of one-story buildings, divided into small rooms. Everyone ate together in a single large dining room.

The Japanese Americans of Bainbridge Island were the first to go to these camps. Many families lost their homes and businesses. It was a time of sadness and suffering.

More than 40 years later, the government admitted that the internment camps were a mistake. Government leaders apologized to the Japanese Americans.

This Japanese American family was moved to an internment camp during the Second World War. Why did Japanese Americans have to move? Do you think this was fair?
(Special Collections Division, University of Washington Libraries)

A civil rights demonstration in Seattle in 1977. (University of Washington *Daily*)

The Civil Rights Movement

However, all Americans did not have an equal share of this **prosperity.** Good jobs often were not open to women and minorities after the war. Many places, such as hotels, theaters, and restaurants, were **segregated.** People of different races lived in separate neighborhoods and went to separate schools. Many members of minority groups could not even vote. They did not have equal rights.

The problems were not as bad in Washington as in some other states. But even here, African American, Hispanic, Asian, and Native Americans experienced prejudice. Many people here joined with other Americans to try to change this.

African Americans were the first to organize. They had big marches. They sat down in segregated buses and restaurants and refused to move. They wrote letters and talked to government leaders. They asked the government to pass new laws.

In 1964, the U.S. government made a very important law. It said that people of all races and cultures must have equal rights. But passing laws does not always make people think differently. Some people were still prejudiced. Change was slow. These laws were an important beginning, but there was still much to be done.

Other groups in Washington have worked for equal rights in similar ways. Native Americans fought for rights that were promised in the treaties. Washington women fought for equal pay. They felt they should earn the same as men doing the same job.

Much progress was made. Hispanic Americans won the right to speak and learn in Spanish. Japanese Americans won an apology for the internment camps of World War II.

As a result of the hard work of all these groups, we now have some good laws. But we still have problems to solve. We must work together to make Washington State a good place for all people to live.

WASHINGTON ARTISTS

This water sculpture was designed by George Tsutakawa.
(Ruth Pelz)

In modern times, Washington State has produced famous artists and performers in many fields. These are a few of them.

MUSIC

Bing Crosby, one of the most popular singers of the 1940s and 1950s, was born in Tacoma.

Jimi Hendrix was perhaps the most important guitarist of his time. He was born and grew up in Seattle's Central Area.

PAINTING

Mark Tobey lived and taught for several years in Seattle. He had great influence on other Washington painters of the postwar years.

Jacob Lawrence was not born in Washington but came here to teach and live. His paintings tell stories of African American history and culture.

SCULPTURE

George Tsutakawa is best known for his water fountain sculptures in Seattle and other cities.

ART SCHOOLS

Nellie Cornish was a pianist. Many artists have had a chance to study or teach in Washington, thanks to Nellie Cornish. She established an art school in Seattle that is nationally known. Several famous painters and performers have spent time at the Cornish College of the Arts, including Mark Tobey.

Boom Times and Beyond

The boom times after World War II went on for almost 25 years. But in the late 1960s, things began to change. The Boeing Company in Seattle lost business. Thousands of airplane workers lost their jobs. A large part of Seattle's population was out of work. Many people left the city. The problems went on for several years. Little by little, Seattle recovered. By the 1980s, the city was growing again.

There were problems in other parts of Washington, too. Changes in the lumber industry caused many loggers to lose their jobs. Times were hard in logging towns around the state. Families in logging towns did not have money to buy clothes, food, or pay their rent.The Tri-cities was another area that lost many jobs. Around the state, many people had to move and find new work.

OLD GROWTH FORESTS— CUT THEM OR KEEP THEM?

When the first settlers came, most of Western Washington was covered with evergreen forests. They were different from most of the forests we see today. Many of the trees were hundreds of years old. Some were so large that pioneer families used a tree stump as a home.

Most of the big trees have been cut down. New forests have grown up to replace some of those lost. But the trees are not as large, and the plants and animals that live in the forests are not the same. The spotted owl is one type of wildlife that needs old growth forests in order to live. There are very few left.

Old growth forests still exist in a few parts of Washington. Some people argue that these forests must be protected. They say, "By saving the last old growth, we are saving part of our history. We are saving some plants and animals that can never be replaced."

However, Washington loggers disagree. "We depend on the forests for our work," they say. "Our communities have already lost many jobs. If we can't cut the old growth, there will be fewer jobs for loggers and mill workers. We will have to leave our homes and schools and friends and go somewhere else to look for different kinds of work. Our families are more important than the trees and the owls."

Our community and government leaders are discussing this problem and trying to find a solution. What is your opinion?

Giant fir log from old-growth forest. (Special Collections Division, University of Washington Libraries)

WORLD'S FAIRS

Two special events helped bring many visitors to Washington in modern times. They were world's fairs. One was held in Seattle and one in Spokane. These summer-long events included foods, displays, and products from all over the world. Some interesting buildings from the fairs still stand in both cities. The Space Needle is the most famous symbol of the Seattle World's Fair. Spokane has a beautiful downtown park and activity center where the fair was held.

This overhead rail system was built for the Seattle World's Fair. (Jeff Murray)

Scientific research is important to Washington's economy. (University of Washington, College of Engineering)

The State Economy

Since World War II there have been many changes in the state economy. The economy has to do with the way people make their living. All the products that people make or buy are part of the economy. So are services, such as car repair, hotels, restaurants, and doctors. An economy is a system of producing and getting the things we need.

In the past, Washington's economy was based on natural

AGRICULTURE PRODUCTION

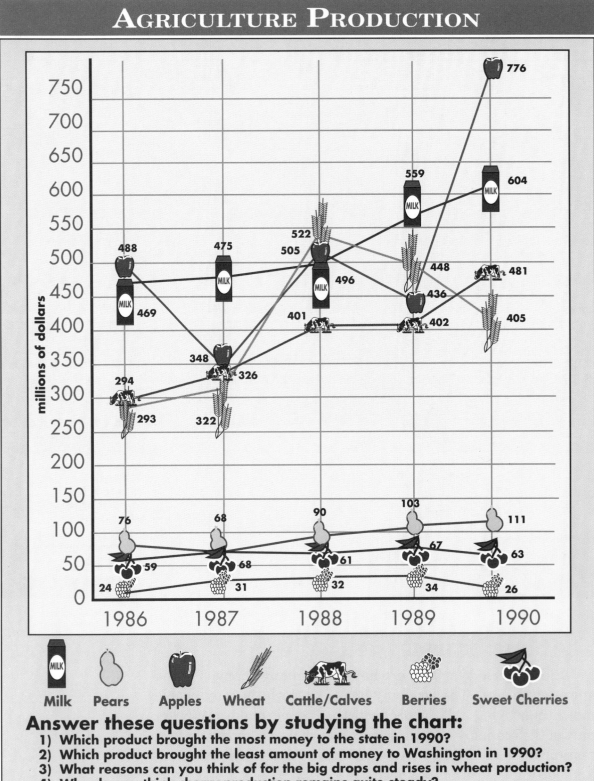

millions of dollars

750
700
650
600
550
500
450
400
350
300
250
200
150
100
50
0

1986 1987 1988 1989 1990

488 475 522 559 604
469   505 496 776
               448 481
294 348   436 405
293 326 401 402
322 90 103 111
76 68   67
59 68 61   63
24 31 32 34 26

Milk   Pears   Apples   Wheat   Cattle/Calves   Berries   Sweet Cherries

Answer these questions by studying the chart:

1) Which product brought the most money to the state in 1990?
2) Which product brought the least amount of money to Washington in 1990?
3) What reasons can you think of for the big drops and rises in wheat production?
4) Why do you think cherry production remains quite steady?

resources. First, there was fur trading. Then forest products became most important. Mills, mines, farming and fishing have provided a large part of the state's jobs.

Natural resources are still very important here. But many other businesses are also important. Some are what we call "high technology" or "high tech." These include computers, electronics, and research. There are also more jobs in services, from restaurants to recreation. This variety has helped make our economy stronger.

On the Farms

Bad weather can cause problems for farmers at any time. The terrible floods of 1990 were an example. They destroyed many crops and dairy cattle.

In general, however, Washington's agriculture has remained strong. Eastern Washington wheat farming communities have been among the wealthiest in the state. The chart on page 128 shows growth and change in some of eastern Washington's most important farm products.

53

The United States has been involved in other wars since World War II. The longest war was in Vietnam. After the war ended, many people moved here from Vietnam and other Southeast Asian countries.
(Photo by Harold McCoy)

The Modern Period

Word Skills

Axis powers   internment   segregated
Allies   suburb   apology
atomic bomb   prosperity   economy
                                      old growth

Things to Know

1. What event caused the United States to enter World War II?

2. Name at least three ways that people in Washington participated in the war effort.

3. What happened to Japanese Americans in the western states during World War II?

4. Name at least three groups of people who helped do wartime work in Washington.

5. Name at least three important changes after the war.

6. Name an important result of the civil rights movement.

7. Describe at least two changes in the state economy in modern times.

What Do You Think?

1. During World War II, women held many kinds of jobs they had never been hired to do before. Why did this happen? Do you think women should have opportunities to do every kind of job today? Why or why not?

2. Pretend you are a person who believed that Japanese Americans should be in camps during the war. Write a statement of your reasons. Then pretend you were a person in these camps. Write a statement telling your opinions about the experience. Then write your own opinion of the event.

3. Do any groups in your community experience prejudice today? What changes are needed? How could the people of your community help bring about these changes?

4. Suppose your community wanted to send a display to a world's fair. What photos or products would you send?

Government

One thing that all people in Washington share is our state government. You may not think about it much, but government is important in many ways.

Government decisions affect all of our lives. You can help make those decisions. The first step is to learn how government works.

This part of the book has two chapters:

Government Then and Now

Government in Washington State.

These chapters will tell you something about the importance of government and how you can take part.

When this family first came to the Pacific Northwest, they lived in the small cabin on the left. They built it themselves from rough boards. They had few neighbors. (Historical Society of Seattle & King County)

Then a city grew up. The family was able to buy the materials to build a big fine house. Their way of life had changed. How did these changes affect the settlers' need for government? (Historical Society of Seattle & King County)

CHAPTER 14

GOVERNMENT THEN AND NOW

Did you ever think about what a government is and why we need it? The early northwest settlers thought about it a great deal. When the first white settlers came, the Pacific Northwest was not part of any country. There was no government here.

This caused many problems. There were no laws and no judges to settle arguments. There were no public schools or services. There were very few roads. There was no army to protect people in case of an attack.

The Pioneers Make Rules

Imagine you are a Washington pioneer. You cross the Oregon Trail with your family and start a farm here. At first, you have no neighbors. You can do pretty much whatever you like. You can cut down trees and plant a garden wherever you want. You can let your cows and horses wander around.

But suppose more and more people come to the region. Some of them settle near you. Now suppose your cows and horses walk through your neighbors' gardens and ruin their crops. Suppose you get your drinking water from a creek, and a neighbor dumps a lot of garbage into it.

How would you solve these problems? Probably you would get together with your neighbors and make some rules. For example, one rule might be that cows and horses have to be fenced in. Another might be that everyone must help keep the creek water clean.

The government has made laws that require children to go to school. This gives everyone an opportunity to learn, like these students in a school dance class. (© 1989 by Jeffrey High Image Productions)

Laws and Services

Making rules, called laws, is one important job done by governments. Laws tell people how they are expected to behave. For example, today's laws say that children must go to school. They say that cars must stop at stop signs.

Laws help stop or settle arguments. They help protect us and the things we own. The government hires police and other workers to make sure that laws are carried out.

Again imagine you are a settler. Imagine there are now 100 families in your area. You may begin to think about other problems in your community. There are no schools. There are no good roads into town. These things are very expensive. One family cannot build roads or build a school alone. But if you and your neighbors all gave a little money, you could build a schoolhouse and hire some teachers. You could hire someone to build roads.

Laws are an important part of government. They tell people how they are expected to behave. Street signs tell drivers what they are supposed to do. (Jeffrey Murray)

Schoolbuildings, books, and teachers are paid for with tax money. (© 1989 by Jeffrey High Image Productions)

STATE REVENUES AND EXPENDITURES

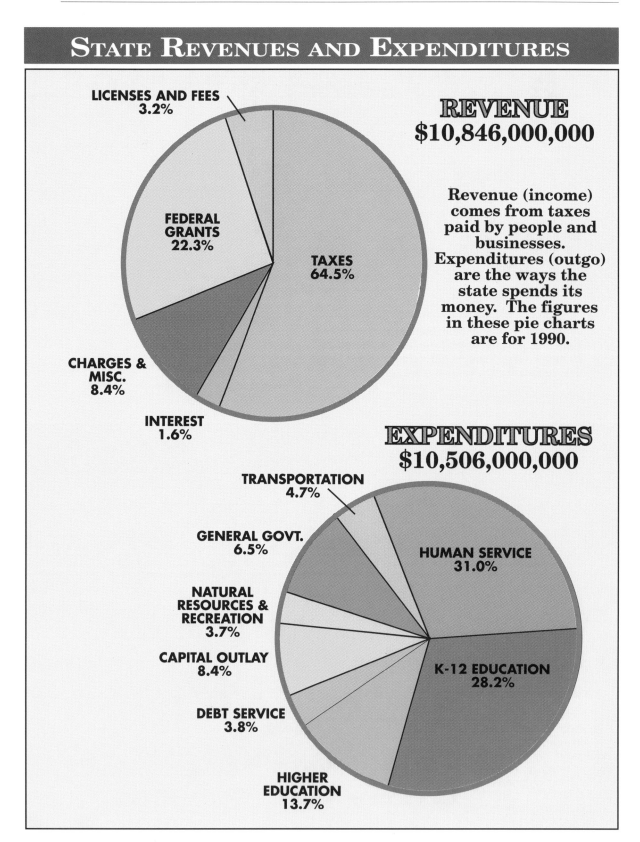

LICENSES AND FEES
3.2%

FEDERAL
GRANTS
22.3%

TAXES
64.5%

CHARGES &
MISC.
8.4%

INTEREST
1.6%

REVENUE
$10,846,000,000

Revenue (income)
comes from taxes
paid by people and
businesses.
Expenditures (outgo)
are the ways the
state spends its
money. The figures
in these pie charts
are for 1990.

EXPENDITURES
$10,506,000,000

TRANSPORTATION
4.7%

GENERAL GOVT.
6.5%

NATURAL
RESOURCES &
RECREATION
3.7%

CAPITAL OUTLAY
8.4%

DEBT SERVICE
3.8%

HUMAN SERVICE
31.0%

K-12 EDUCATION
28.2%

HIGHER
EDUCATION
13.7%

Providing roads and schools is another important job of the government. In order to pay for these things, governments collect some money from everyone in an area. This money is called **taxes.** Taxes pay for our government services, such as schools, judges, and police.

Why Is Voting Important?

In pioneer days, everyone in a community could help make the rules. They could all meet together and make decisions about community problems. This is not possible in today's big towns and cities. It is not possible for all the people in a state or nation to meet and make decisions.

In the United States, all people can still take part in government. But today, we do this in a different way. Instead of making all the laws ourselves, we choose a few people to do this job. We choose these people by voting at **elections.** Every U.S. citizen over 18 years old can vote. All adults can help choose our government leaders.

Choosing a Leader

If you were old enough to vote, whom would you choose? You would probably choose someone who shares your beliefs about important issues.

Suppose you believe that we need more parks. You would want to vote for someone who also shares this belief. That person could help see that the government makes more parks. If the person elected does not do this, you could vote for someone else at the next election.

Government leaders **represent** the voters. When you represent people, this means you speak for them. If the leaders do a good job, the voters will probably elect them again. If the voters are unhappy, they may choose other people to be their leaders. For this reason, the leaders care what voters think.

Voting is important. It is the main way to take part in government. It is the main way to make government meet our needs.

Voters can talk to government leaders. They can write letters and share their ideas. This is important because it helps the leaders do a better job of representing voters.

BECOMING A VOTER

All U.S. citizens over age 18 can vote. To become a voter, you must **register.** This is a simple process. You just fill in a form with your name and address. You can register at most libraries, schools, and government offices after your 18th birthday. You will then receive a voter registration card and a notice in the mail. This will tell you where you can vote each election day.

Government Then and Now

Word Skills

service   election   register
tax   represent

Things to Know

1. Why did the pioneers want a government?
2. How can Americans take part in government?
3. Why must government leaders pay attention to what the voters want?

What Do You Think?

1. What are some government services that you use? List as many as you can.

2. Do you think it is a good idea for voters to elect leaders to represent them? Or should voters be able to make more government decisions themselves? Explain your answer.

3. For nearly 100 years of U.S. history, only white men could vote. Do you think this was a good idea? Why is it important for other groups in our country to vote?

4. Do you think 18 is a good age to start voting? Should younger people be allowed to vote? Explain your answer.

140

STATE, COUNTY, AND CITY GOVERNMENTS DO MANY THINGS TO MEET THE NEEDS OF THE PEOPLE.

Picking up garbage is an important government service. Some Washington governments help with recycling. This is a scene from the Jefferson County Recycling Center. (Eileen Barron.)

Fire protection is a service provided by city or county government. (Ruth Pelz)

CHAPTER 15

Executive Branch
Sees that laws are carried out

Judicial Branch
Interprets the laws

Legislative Branch
Makes the laws

GOVERNMENT IN WASHINGTON STATE

The U.S. system of government has three main parts, or branches. The first branch makes the laws. The second branch carries out the laws. And the third branch makes decisions about laws. The names and duties of these branches are listed on the chart.

Here is an example of how this type of government works. Suppose your state is thinking about making a new park. The legislative branch, the lawmakers, study the idea. They talk to people about the new park and discuss it among themselves. Then they vote. If a majority of the lawmakers vote yes, they make a new law.

Then the executive branch takes over. This branch will carry out the law. It will buy the land and see that the park is built.

Now suppose there is a problem in the park. Suppose some people go hunting on park land. Perhaps they hunted here before this was a park and feel they should be able to continue. The park leaders disagree.

This is where the judicial branch comes in. It is the branch that includes our courts and judges. This branch makes decisions about the law.

Judges settle arguments about the law. They help decide if a person has broken the law, and they decide exactly what laws mean. The judge would study the laws and their history and make a decision about who is right. In this example, a judge would listen to the hunters and the park leaders.

WILLIAM O. DOUGLAS

William O. Douglas had a difficult start in life. He was sick as a child. His father died, and young Bill and his mother were left quite poor.

William Douglas spent his school years in the Yakima Valley. He loved to hike in the Cascade Mountains, and he studied hard so that he could go to college. He became a lawyer and then a judge. Later, he became a judge in the highest court of the country, the U.S. Supreme Court.

All his life, he loved the natural environment of the Pacific Northwest. He hiked all around the region and wrote about the land and wildlife of the Northwest. He wrote about the importance of protecting our special environment.

William O. Douglas believed strongly that all Americans should have equal rights. As a Supreme Court judge, he worked to protect the rights of all people in our country.

William O. Douglas became a judge in the nation's highest court. (Fabian Bachrach)

Jim McDermott serves as our state's representative to the Federal Government in the House of Representatives.

Jennifer Dunn is a member of the U.S. House of Representatives serving on behalf of Washington.

Federal Government

Did you know that you are part of several governments? First there is the government for the entire country. Everyone in the United States is part of it. This is the federal government. The center of federal government is in Washington, D.C.

The federal government makes laws for people all over the country. For example, federal laws say that all Americans have certain rights. We have the right to speak freely. We have the right to choose our religion. All citizens have equal rights.

The federal government has special importance in Washington State. A very large part of our land is owned or controlled by the federal government. This land includes our national parks, national forests, Indian reservations, and much of the irrigated farmland.

The state legislature meets here, in the *capitol* building. This is not a misspelling. A *capital* is the center of government. Olympia is Washington's capital. The *capitol* is the building where lawmakers meet. (Jeffrey High)

State Government

Each state also has its own government. This government makes laws that have to do with the lands and people of the state. For example, some state laws are about crime. Others have to do with how businesses may be run. The license plates for our cars come from state government. So does part of the money for schools and colleges.

The center of Washington State government is in Olympia. This is our state capital, just as Washington, D.C., is the capital of our country. The main offices of all three branches of government are in the capital city.

WASHINGTON COUNTIES

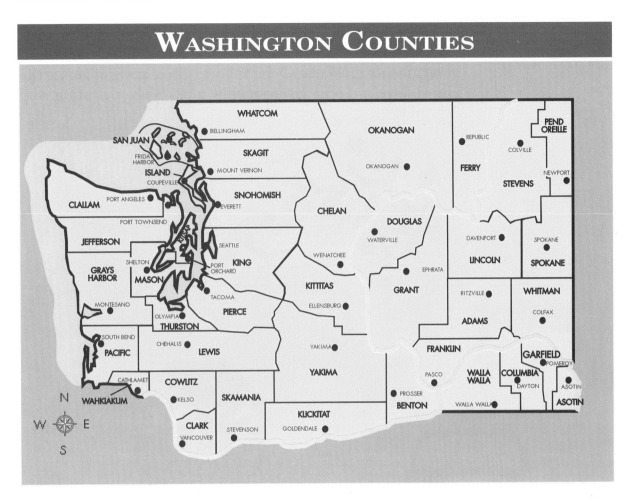

Local Government

There is one other level of government. It is called local government. Local governments serve small areas. The main example is county government.

Washington State is divided into 39 counties. Each county has its own government, centered in the county seat. You can find them on the map.

County governments make laws and provide services for people in the county. Police and fire protection are two important examples.

In some parts of the state, these local services are provided by city governments. If you live in a city, you are part of both a city and a county government.

Everyone is also part of another kind of local government, called districts. For example, we all live in a school district. The school district runs the schools in your area.

146

Federal, state, and local are the three levels of government. Federal government is the highest level. All state and local governments must obey federal laws. Local government is the lowest level. Local governments must obey the state and federal laws.

LOCAL GOVERNMENT PROVIDES THESE AND OTHER SERVICES

Our Governments and Our Future

The governments of our state and nation will have many important decisions to make in the coming years. There will be many choices that have to do with the natural environment. There will be decisions about our schools. Senators and representatives will make many decisions about taxes and how to spend them.

You can help make these decisions. You can begin now by learning about them. You can study the choices that must be made. You can talk to people about them and listen to the news. You can form your own opinions and help to bring about the decisions you want.

When you reach the age of 18, you can register to vote. Learning about government and taking part in it are important responsibilities of all U.S. citizens.

Police officers are an important kind of local government worker. This police woman is talking to a class about drugs. (Jeffrey High)

How will we use Washington's forest resources? (Therese Ogle)

How will we keep our air and water clean? How can we help protect the environment? (Seattle Aquarium)

THESE ARE SOME DECISIONS FACING OUR GOVERNMENTS IN THE 21ST CENTURY. WHAT CHOICES DO YOU THINK WE SHOULD MAKE?

- How to use Washington's forest resources
- Solving the transportation problems in Washington cities
- Providing health care for all
- Cleaning up pollution
- Dealing with population growth
- Protecting the civil rights of all people

Government in Washington State

Word Skills

branch	federal	county seat
legislative	capital	district
executive	capitol	senator
judicial	county	representative

Things to Know

1. What are the three branches of government? What are the responsibilities of each branch?
2. What are the three levels of government?
3. Name the capitals of Washington State and the United States.
4. What county do you live in? What is your county seat?

What Do You Think?

1. The federal government prints our money and oversees our post offices. What might happen if each state provided these services on its own?
2. Federal laws say that all people have equal rights. Could a state make a law saying that some people do not have equal rights? Why or why not?
3. What are some important decisions facing your community? How can you learn about these issues?

View from stone tower at the top of Mt. Constitution on Orcas Island. (Washington State Tourism Division)

Washington State ferries transport people and cars across Puget Sound. (The Port of Seattle)

A CLOSER LOOK

In the first part of this book, you learned the names of the five main parts of our state. They are the:

- **Coast**
- **Western Lowlands**
- **Cascade Mountains**
- **Columbia Plateau**
- **Okanogan Highlands**

In this section, we will take a closer look at each of these parts. We will learn a little about the things to see and do around Washington. We will look at the people of the state, the way they live and the kinds of work they do. There is one chapter for each part of the state.

As you read these chapters, remember what you have learned about the geography and history of the state. These things will help you understand how people live in Washington today.

THE COASTAL REGION

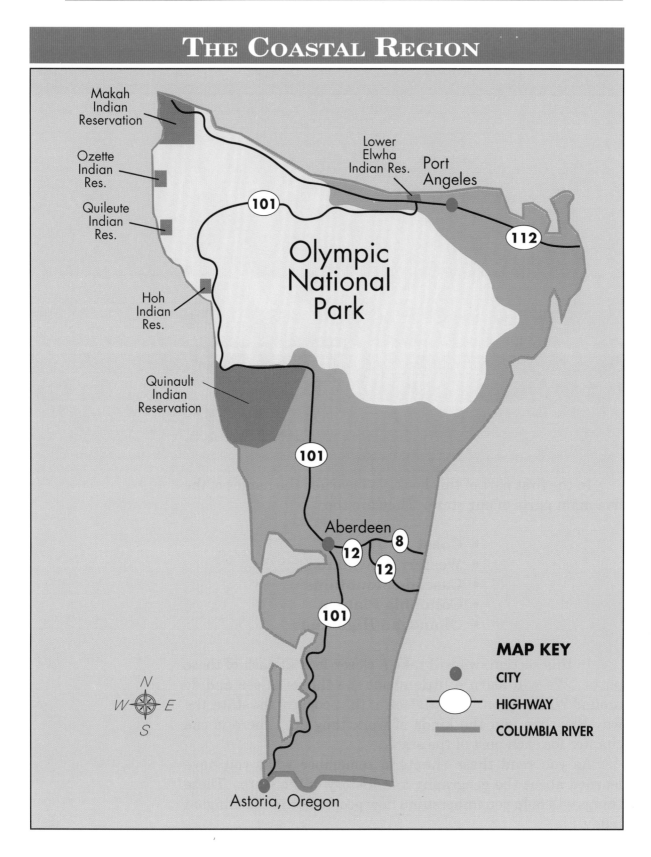

Makah Indian Reservation

Ozette Indian Res.

Quileute Indian Res.

Hoh Indian Res.

Quinault Indian Reservation

Lower Elwha Indian Res.

Port Angeles

101

Olympic National Park

112

101

Aberdeen

12

8

12

101

101

Astoria, Oregon

N
W · E
S

MAP KEY

● CITY

◯ HIGHWAY

▬ COLUMBIA RIVER

CHAPTER 16

WASHINGTON'S COASTAL AREAS

Have you ever taken a walk along Washington's coast? The chances are good that the day was wet and cloudy.

The Washington coast is one of the rainiest places in the whole United States. Some places get almost 150 inches (375 centimeters) of rain each year. That is more than 12 feet. It is higher than the ceiling above you! It is nearly three times the amount of rain that falls on Seattle and nine times the amount that falls on Spokane.

Damp, mild, ocean winds blow daily over the coastal lands. The weather changes fast. Sometimes there is bright sunshine, but it is usually cloudy or rainy for at least part of the day.

ANIMALS UNDER THE TIDES

If you have ever visited the ocean, you probably know about **tides.** The level of the ocean is constantly changing. It rises for several hours, until the high tide is reached. The water comes high up on the beach. Then the level drops again. This happens twice each day.

A lot of animals live on Washington beaches under the tides. They live under water part of the day. During the low tide, they may not be under water. This is a good time to examine them. You may look at them and even touch them, but you cannot take live animals from the beach. State and national parks protect our wildlife for all visitors to enjoy.

154

Sea stars, or starfish, come in many colors and sizes. They eat clams and other shellfish.
(Seattle Aquarium)

Several kinds of crabs are found along Washington's coast.
(Seattle Aquarium)

A trail through the rain forest in Olympic National Park. (National Park Service)

THREE NATIONAL PARKS

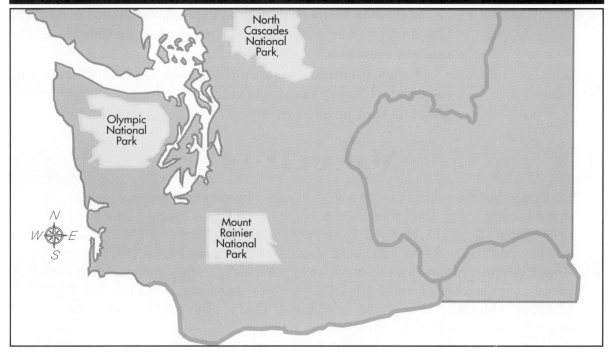

North Cascades National Park,

Olympic National Park

Mount Rainier National Park

N W E S

Olympic National Park

This wet and mild climate is very good for trees. Thick forests cover much of the land along the coast. A very special kind of forest, called a rain forest, is found on the Olympic Peninsula. It is thick and green and full of many kinds of plants. You can visit Washington's rain forest at Olympic National Park.

There are many things to do in the park and many interesting things to see. On the ocean beaches, you can search for interesting rocks and shells. You can climb on huge driftwood logs that have been carried ashore by the ocean.

Just beyond the beaches, the forests begin. There are many hiking trails through the forests and mountains of Olympic National Park. There are lakes for swimming and boating. There is good fishing in the clear mountain streams.

The national parks were created to preserve places of special beauty. We are lucky to have three in Washington State.

Working Along the Coast

Every year, people come to the Washington coast on vacation. Tourism is an important industry. It provides many jobs for the people who live here.

Most jobs in the coastal area depend on natural resources. Catching fish and other seafoods and packaging these foods for sale are examples.

Forest products make up the most important industry of the coast. It takes many workers to cut down trees and make products that people can use.

MAKAH DAYS

Remember the village of Ozette? A closely related tribe, the Makah, still live in the coastal area. The little fishing town of Neah Bay is located on the Makah reservation. So is a wonderful museum that includes many of the treasures of Ozette. Each year, the Makah host a special festival called Makah Days. Native Americans from around the region come to participate. Among the highlights are races of large dugout canoes. Other coastal reservations include the Hoh, Quileute, Quinault, Shoalwater, and Lower Elwha. There are more than 20 reservations in Western Washington.

Packing fish for market is an important job. The fish must be canned or frozen speedily and at the proper temperature to keep out harmful bacteria.
(Port of Seattle)

158

Loggers have the first job. They go into the forest and cut down trees. In the past, this work was done by hand, with axes and saws. Teams of oxen dragged the logs out of the forest.

Today, loggers have many machines to help them. They use chain saws to cut down trees, trim off the branches, and cut the trees into long sections. These trimmed trees are called logs. Other machines drag, or skid, the logs to a loading area and lift them onto trucks.

LOGGING CHANGES

When pioneers came to Western Washington, nearly all the land was covered by forests. For farmers, this meant hard work to clear and plow their fields. For sawmills and lumber companies, it meant plenty of business.

With forests all around them, people grew careless. They wasted a lot of wood. They cut down huge forests without planting new trees. They never worried about the effects on the natural environment.

In time, logging technology changed and so did people's attitudes. Laws were passed to protect forest resources. Some companies began planting trees. Today, little wood is wasted. Almost every part of the log is used.

In recent times, concern for our environment has grown stronger. The government has had to make difficult decisions about how to use our forests. More decisions will be needed in the future. You will probably have a chance to help make those decisions. So it is important to learn about our forest resources and how we use them.

Planting new trees to replace a forest that has been cut down. This is one way to protect our forest resources. (Weyerhaeuser Corporation)

Giant rolls of paper are manufactured at this Washington paper mill. What natural resource is used to make paper? (Weyerhaeuser Corporation)

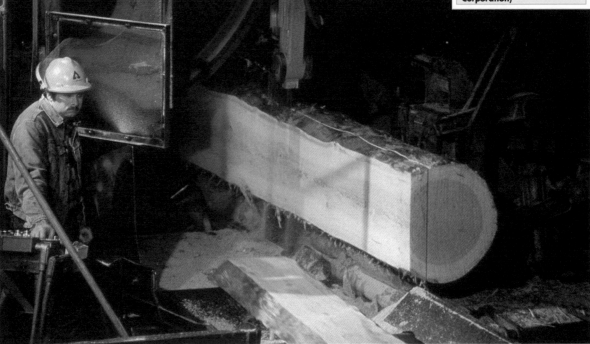

Cutting logs at a sawmill. (Weyerhaeuser Corporation)

The trucks then take many of the logs to sawmills. Here, the logs may float in ponds of water until they are used. Then long, moving belts carry the logs into the mill.

At the sawmill, the first step is removing the bark of the tree. This is often done with powerful jets of water. Next, the log is carried back and forth through the sharp blades of a saw. Computers help plan how to cut the log so that all the wood is used. The boards are dried and then cut smooth to make finished lumber. Then, of course, the lumber is used to make many products.

A World of Wood Products

Look around you. How many things in your home or school are made of wood?

Did you include paper on your list? Paper is made from wood at another kind of mill. Here, chips of wood and sawdust are mixed with water and chemicals. This mixture, called pulp, is used to make paper, cardboard, and other products. You can find pulp and paper mills in many Washington cities.

Plywood is another interesting and important wood product. It is something like a wood sandwich. To make plywood, a log is spun around and around. A special blade cuts a thin layer of wood as the log spins. It is something like peeling an apple. Then these thin layers are stacked up and glued together. Plywood is stronger and less expensive than lumber. In many houses, plywood is used to make cabinets, floors, and walls.

Chipboard and particle board are other common building materials. They are made of wood chips or sawdust, pressed tightly together.

Washington's Coastal Areas

Word Skills

tide
rain forest
driftwood
lumber
plywood

Things to Know

1. Why do trees grow so well along Washington's coast?
2. Name at least three jobs or businesses of the coast that depend on natural resources.
3. Name two forest products and tell how they are made.

What Do You Think?

1. Why do areas with a lot of rain have a lot of rivers? What would happen if water could not run off the land?
2. Many people in Washington have jobs in the forest products industry. If more trees were cut down, there might be even more jobs. Do you think this is a good idea? Why or why not?
3. Some places along the east side of the Olympic Mountains get very little rain each year. Can you explain why?

THE WESTERN LOWLANDS

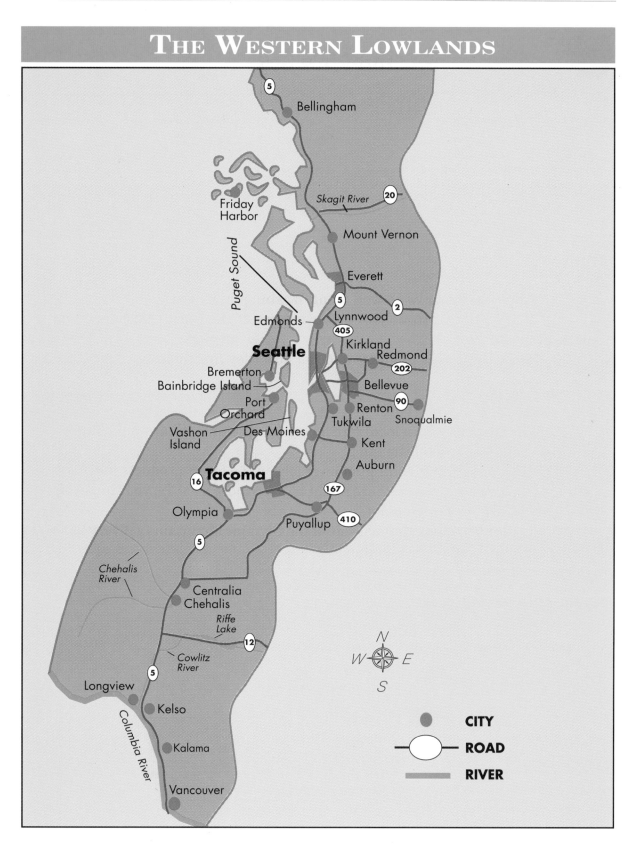

CHAPTER 17

THE WESTERN LOWLANDS

Where in Washington can you find:
- the largest room in the world?
- the second longest island in the United States?
- three of the world's very few floating bridges?
- more boats than any other place its size?
- a children's museum and a children's theater?
- major league sports?
- miles of tulip and daffodil fields?
- foods from Bolivia, Pakistan, Austria, Ethiopia, and dozens of other nations?
- growing pollution problems and terrible traffic jams?

You can find all these things in the Western Lowlands. The Lowlands have more people and more activities than any other part of the state. Washington's biggest cities have choices, advantages, and problems common to big cities everywhere.

164

These cars and trucks have come by ship from Japan. What ocean must you cross to travel from Japan to Washington State? (Port of Seattle)

This dock worker is an important link between water transportation and ground transportation. (Port of Seattle)

Cities Need Transportation

Many things have helped the Lowlands cities grow. The first is transportation. Seattle, Tacoma, Bellingham, Everett, and other cities have deep-water ports on Puget Sound. Vancouver, Kalama, and Longview have ports on the Columbia River.

These ports were especially important in the early days. Pioneers depended on boats for nearly all their transportation. Shipping and trade are still important businesses in the Lowlands. Seattle and Tacoma especially are centers of international trade.

Today, the big cities are also served by railroads, airports, and highways. These cities are busy day and night. People and products are constantly moving from place to place.

This Boeing plant in Everett contains the largest single room in the world. (The Boeing Company)

Cities Need Jobs

Cities need jobs in order to grow. The Lowlands cities are centers of manufacturing, services, government, and trade. They have many businesses and provide thousands of jobs.

Airplane manufacturing is the largest industry in the state. The Boeing Company has plants in Seattle, Everett, and Renton. Many smaller companies in this area also make airplane parts.

Computers and electronics make up another fast-growing manufacturing industry. If your family has a computer, the chances are good that some of the software was made by a Washington company.

There are many other kinds of jobs in the cities. There are office jobs in banks and other businesses. There are service jobs in restaurants, shops, and hotels. There are construction jobs. Many people work on army, navy, and air force bases. Large numbers of people—especially in Seattle and Olympia—work in government offices. And that is just a beginning.

In 1990 Bremerton, Washington, was voted the nation's "most livable city." (Seattle has won this title in the past.) Why do many people find the Lowlands cities a nice place to live? (Bremerton/Kitsap County Visitor & Convention Bureau)

A Pleasant Place to Live

Jobs have helped bring many people to the cities. So has the pleasant environment of the Lowlands. The climate is not too hot or too cold. The setting is beautiful. There are wonderful views of mountains, lakes, rivers, islands, and Puget Sound.

And there are plenty of interesting things to do. The large cities have theaters, symphonies, rock concerts, and sports events. They have libraries, museums, and schools of many kinds. There are biking, boating, and skiing areas nearby.

Urban Growth, Urban Problems

Look at the map of central Puget Sound on page 162. There are many cities here. Seattle is by far the largest. But only about one quarter of the people live in Seattle itself. It is often more useful to talk about the Seattle metropolitan area. A metropolitan area includes one or two central cities and their suburbs. The two largest metropolitan areas of the Western Lowlands are located around Seattle, Washington and Portland, Oregon.

People driving in the cities often get stuck in heavy traffic. What problems does traffic create? (Jeffrey High)

Each community in a metropolitan area is different from the others in some ways. However, they share common advantages and problems. Perhaps the most obvious problem in the many metropolitan areas is traffic.

Every day, people fill the metropolitan streets and highways, commuting between home and work. Because of this traffic there are more accidents. The trip takes longer. People get angry. And the air pollution gets much worse.

Although most people used to work in Seattle, this has begun to change. Many new industries are located in the suburbs. Bellevue and Redmond are leading centers of the state's high technology businesses, for example. During the morning and afternoon rush hour, streets are crowded in every direction!

Urban, or city, growth has brought advantages to the Lowlands cities. But it has also brought problems. Washington cities face many difficult decisions about these problems, now and in the years ahead.

Farming and Other Rural Activities

Not everyone in the Western Lowlands lives in cities, of course. In fact, one of the state's richest farming areas is the Skagit River Valley. This broad, flat valley in the northern Lowlands produces many crops. Tulips and daffodils are the most famous. Every spring, fields of colorful flowers stretch as far as the eye can see.

The rich soils and mild climate of the Skagit Valley are also good for vegetables. Peas, carrots, cauliflower, broccoli, and other crops are raised here. Some are grown for their seeds. Some are canned or frozen. Other vegetables are sold fresh.

The Cowlitz and Chehalis river valleys are also farming

regions. Many kinds of berries are grown in the Western Lowlands. Dairy cattle and chickens are also raised on Lowlands farms.

Southwest Washington is an important logging area. The port cities on the Columbia River are centers of the state's pulp and paper industry.

At Pike Place Market you can see people, food, and gift items from many parts of the world.
(Pike Place Market Preservation and Development Authority)

Ethnic Groups

The Western Lowlands population is larger and more diverse than any other part of the state. People of many different ethnic groups have helped develop the Lowlands communities. Here are a few interesting facts:

• The town of Centralia was founded by an African American. His name was George Washington.

• Gig Harbor was founded by a Yugoslavian fisherman named Sam Jerisch. He built the town's first dock, factory, and warehouse.

• Kalama and Friday Harbor were both named for Hawaiians who worked for the Hudson's Bay Company.

• There are many small Indian reservations around Puget Sound. On the Suquamish Reservation, you can visit Chief Sealth's grave and a tribal museum. The Lummi Reservation includes an underwater farm where fish and oysters are raised.

• When the Pike Place Market first opened in Seattle, most of the stands were run by Italian and Japanese farmers. You can still visit this famous market to buy gifts and fresh foods. Today the shops sell products from many world countries, as well as from Washington State.

Sailing is a popular activity in the San Juans. Even just watching the boats is fun. This is a port at Friday Harbor. (Washington State Tourism Division)

The Western Lowlands

Word Skills

port
international trade
manufacturing

electronics
software
metropolitan area

commute
urban
diverse
ethnic group

Things to Know

1. In which part of the state do most people live?
2. Name at least five industries of the Western Lowlands.
3. Name three things that have brought people to the Lowlands cities.
4. Name two problems facing the big Lowlands cities.
5. Name at least five agricultural products of the Western Lowlands.

What Do You Think?

1. What things do cities need in order to grow? List all the things you can think of.

2. What makes a city livable? What things do you think the "most livable city" should have?

3. What kind of job would you like to have when you grow up? Could you find this work in the Western Lowlands?

THE CASCADE MOUNTAINS

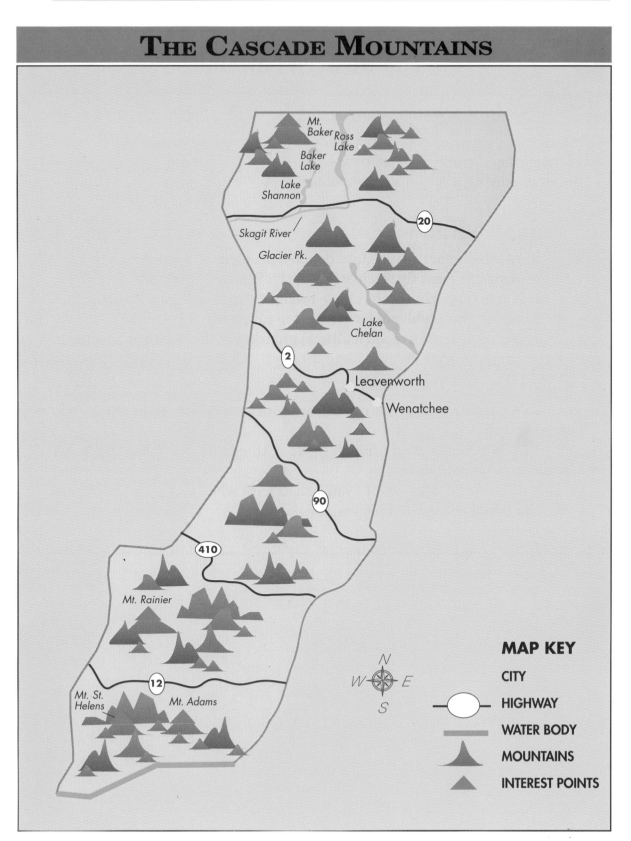

Mt. Baker

Ross Lake

Baker Lake

Lake Shannon

20

Skagit River

Glacier Pk.

Lake Chelan

2

Leavenworth

Wenatchee

90

410

Mt. Rainier

12

Mt. St. Helens

Mt. Adams

N
W E
S

MAP KEY

CITY

HIGHWAY

WATER BODY

MOUNTAINS

INTEREST POINTS

CHAPTER 18

THE CASCADE MOUNTAINS

Mount Saint Helens, erupting.
(U.S. Department of Interior;
U.S. Geological Survey,
Cascades Volcano
Observatory)

On the morning of May 18, 1980, many people in Washington were awakened by the sound of an explosion. Mount Saint Helens had erupted.

For weeks, there had been signs of danger. A series of small earthquakes shook the land. Towers of steam rose from the mountain top. Scientists could tell that the mountain was swelling.

Everyone was told to leave the area. Most people did. Still, no one knew exactly what might happen, or when.

On May 18, they found out. A big chunk of the mountain

slipped downward. Then came the explosion. It was stronger than the force of a thousand bombs. A burst of burning gas rushed down the mountainside, killing all living things in its path. Snows on the mountain melted and mixed with dirt. Great rivers of mud knocked down trees, carried away houses, and buried the land. Tons of mud filled up nearby rivers, causing high floods.

The force of the eruption broke rocks into fine gray dust called ash. A fountain of ash shot upward, rising nine miles into the sky.

The winds were blowing from the west that day, as they usually do in this area. Those winds blew the ash over eastern Washington. The air was thick with gray dust. In the middle of the day, eastern Washington was dark as night. Highways, schools, and businesses were closed. People had to stay indoors. Soon many parts of the state were buried under inches of ash.

Washington's Famous Volcanoes

Mount Saint Helens is a volcano. So are the four highest peaks of the state: Mount Rainier, Mount Adams, Mount Baker, and Glacier Peak. All have erupted before and will probably erupt again. Mount Saint Helens has had many smaller eruptions since 1980. Studies at Mount Saint Helens may help scientists predict when other eruptions will happen.

Even when they are quiet, Washington's volcanoes are famous. They are known as wonderful places to visit and see.

Mount Rainier is a great place for hikes and nature walks. (Washington State Tourism Division)

The best known is probably Mount Rainier. It is the tallest mountain of the Cascades. Its beautiful, snowy peak rises above the Seattle-Tacoma metropolitan area, the biggest population center of the state.

Mount Rainier's special beauty was noted by explorers and settlers on Puget Sound. It became the first national park in Washington. It was also one of the first national parks in the United States.

Today, Mount Rainier National Park offers attractions for every kind of visitor. Skilled mountain climbers find the peak a challenge. Hikers and backpackers can explore dozens of trails. They can camp by rushing streams and clear, cold mountain lakes. They can roam meadows of wildflowers in summer, or explore the mountain on skis in winter. But you do not need to be an athlete to enjoy the park. There are also miles of high mountain roads with splendid views that can be explored by car.

Inside this dam are giant machines called generators. As water flows down through the dam, it makes the generators turn. This creates electricity.
(Seattle City Light)

Power from Mountain Rivers

Washington's newest national park is about 150 miles north of Mount Rainier. One interesting attraction of North Cascades National Park is its large, high-elevation lakes. You can find them on the map on page 172. These lakes were not formed by nature. They were created by dams. The dams produce electricity, one of the Cascade Mountains' most important products.

Each year, melted snow fills the rivers that tumble down the steep slopes of the Cascades. This fast-flowing water is very powerful. It is one of the state's valuable resources.

In the past, that power was used to run sawmills and flour mills. Today, it is used to make hydroelectricity. (Hydro means having to do with water.) Washington's many hyordroelectric dams supply electric power to homes and factories of the Pacific Northwest.

Two Kinds of Forests

You have learned that the east and west sides of the Cascades have different climates. They also have different natural vegetation. The forests of the western slopes are thick. Mosses, ferns, and bushes grow beneath the trees. Hemlocks, firs, and cedar trees grow in the damp marine forests of the western Cascades.

Ross Lake, North Cascades (National Park Service)

Skiing is one popular sport that attracts people to the Cascades. (Tacoma Visitor/Convention Bureau)

The town of Leavenworth, Washington, has been built to look like a town in the mountains of Germany. (Therese Ogle)

The eastern slopes get much less rain, and the forests are not as thick. Not as many plants grow on the forest floor. The most important tree of the eastern forests is the ponderosa pine.

The highest lands of the Cascades have no trees at all. Very high on the mountaintops it is too cold for trees to grow. The elevation where the trees stop is called the tree line.

Crossing the Cascades

The Cascade Mountains are wonderful to visit, but not many people live in the mountains all year. The climate of the Cascade Mountains is cold. The land is rough. It is hard to build roads or buildings on steep slopes. It is hard to get from place to place. For these reasons, Washington's biggest cities are all located in other parts of the state.

Only a few roads cross the Cascade Mountains. Even these roads may be closed by snow in the winter. It snows a lot in these mountains, especially on the western slopes. Snoqualmie Pass gets almost 40 feet (about 12 meters) of snow each year!

The Columbia Basin

The only low elevation route across the Cascades is along the Columbia River. It is the only river that crosses the Cascade Range.

On a large map of the state, find the Columbia River. Then find some rivers that flow down the east side of the Cascades. You can see that they all flow into the Columbia. (Some flow first into a larger river and this larger river flows into the Columbia.) Small rivers that flow into a larger river are called **tributaries.** The Columbia carries all this water to the Pacific Ocean.

In this way, the Columbia River is something like the drain in a sink or bathtub. The name for all the land drained by a river and its tributaries is **basin.** The Columbia Basin is very large. It includes most of the northwest states and part of other states and Canada.

Strong winds blow up the Columbia River where it crosses the Cascade Mountains. This makes the area a good place for wind surfing.
(© Jeffrey High Image Productions)

The Cascade Mountains

Word Skills

hydroelectricity
tree line
tributary
basin

Things to Know

1. What happened to Mount Saint Helens in 1980?
2. Name four other volcanoes of Washington State.
3. What two national parks are located in Washington's Cascade Mountains?
4. Briefly explain how hydroelectricity is produced.
5. Describe the natural vegetation on the east and west slopes of the Cascades.

What Do You Think?

1. On a map of Washington, find at least four lakes that were formed by dams. How can you tell?
2. In the Pacific Northwest, we get electricity from hydroelectric dams, nuclear power plants, and plants that burn coal or other fuels. Some people are also trying out ways of generating electricity from sunlight. How do each of these methods affect our environment? Learn more about these methods and compare them.
3. Would you like to live in the Cascade Mountains all year? Why or why not?

THE COLUMBIA PLATEAU

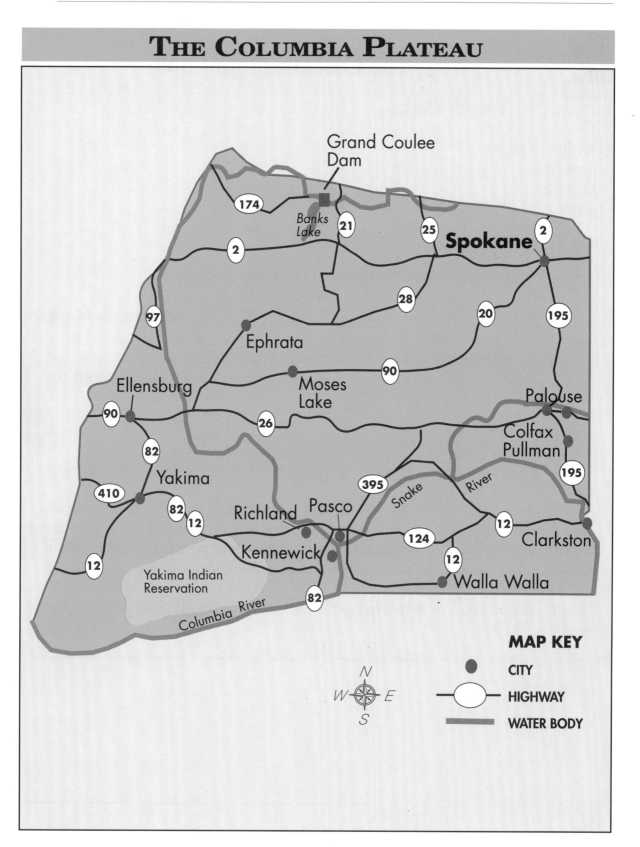

Grand Coulee Dam

174

Banks Lake

21

25

Spokane

2

2

28

97

20

195

Ephrata

90

Ellensburg

Moses Lake

Palouse

90

Colfax
Pullman

26

195

82

Yakima

410

82

12

395

Snake River

Richland

Pasco

12

Clarkston

12

Kennewick

124

195

Yakima Indian
Reservation

12

Walla Walla

Columbia River

82

MAP KEY

● CITY

⬭ HIGHWAY

▬ WATER BODY

N
W E
S

The Wenatchee Valley is famous for apples. Washington grows more apples than any state in the country, and a lot of them come from the Wenatchee area. The climate of this valley is just right for apple trees. Northwest farmers raise many kinds of apples. This one, called Washington Red Delicious, is the most famous. **(Washington Apple Commission)**

THE COLUMBIA PLATEAU

The Columbia Plateau is a large geographic area. It includes most of eastern Washington and parts of Oregon and Idaho as well.

It includes some of the driest land in the Pacific Northwest. Lands with less than 10 inches (25 centimeters) of precipitation each year are deserts. Look at the map on page 23 to see where the deserts of Washington are located.

The Columbia Plateau climate is too dry for trees. The natural vegetation ranges from grassland to desert sagebrush.

But in some places, the vegetation is different. If you took a plane ride over the Columbia Plateau, you might notice something unusual. Below you, in the midst of the brown desert, are patches of bright green. Some are square, like pieces of a quilt. Some are circles. And a few seem to be long, green threads.

On the Columbia Plateau there are thousands of acres of orchards. Besides apples, other orchard crops are pears, peaches, apricots, and plums. (Washington Apple Commission)

Can you guess why the vegetation is different in these areas? The reason is water. If you flew closer, you would see that the long, green lines are rivers. Many plants grow along the rivers' edge.

Long, long ago, farmers learned that they could grow plants in dry lands by bringing water to them. This is called irrigation.

Many types of irrigation are used on the Columbia Plateau. One type uses a long sprinkler that moves around a central point. This makes the green circles you can see from the air.

Calming the Columbia

The water for irrigation comes from rivers. Much of it comes from the state's largest river, the Columbia.

The Columbia is much calmer now than in the time of William Clark. The reason is dams. There now are several high dams across the river. Behind them, the water is deep. The old rapids are now under many feet of water.

The dams on the Columbia River produce hydroelectricity. They also help store water to be used for irrigation. A place

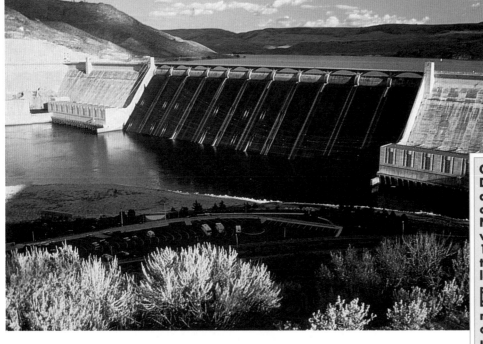

Literature

The Awesome Columbia River

Today, the Columbia River looks deep and peaceful. It used to look quite different. These are some things the explorer William Clark wrote as he journeyed down the Columbia in 1805.

"October 20th: We passed a very bad rapid, a chain of rocks ... nearly choking the river.

"October 21st: After passing this rapid, we proceeded on past another rapid at five miles lower down.

"October 25th: This channel is through a hard, rough, black rock, from 50 to 100 yards wide. [The water is] swelling and boiling in a most tremendous manner.

"October 31st: Very considerable rapid, at which place the waves are incredibly high ..."

This wheat will turn golden yellow in the fall, telling the farmer that the wheat is ready for harvest. What foods that you eat contain wheat? (Photo © Jeffrey High)

where water is stored is called a **reservoir.** Banks Lake, near Grand Coulee Dam, is a large and important reservoir for the Columbia Plateau. It stores water for people living on the Columbia Plateau.

What is Dry Farming?

Wheat is the most important crop of the Columbia Plateau. It is grown in several areas.

In the Palouse Hills of southeastern Washington, the soils are rich and deep. Many Palouse farmers plant only part of their land with wheat each year. The other part just sits there. Rain falls on the unplanted land and is stored in the deep soil.

The next year, this land is planted with wheat. Wheat plants have very long roots. These roots can reach into the soil and use the moisture that is stored there. The plants get part of the moisture they need from this year's rain. They get the rest from the soil.

This method of growing wheat is called **dry farming.** In other areas, wheat fields are irrigated.

A Year on a Washington Wheat Farm

A farmer's yearly work varies from place to place and crop to crop. This is a typical year on a Palouse wheat farm.

Winter is a quiet time. It is a time for repairing farm machines and planning the next year's activities.

In March, the spring plowing and planting begins. Farmers spray the land with weed killer. In May and June, they work on the land that has not been planted. They get it ready for the next year's crop.

By late summer, this year's crop is ripe. The harvest starts in late July and ends in August. Harvesting the wheat and getting it to market is a big job.

September is the month for putting in fertilizers and new seeds. In October, the weeds are sprayed again. In November, there is more plowing. Then it is back to fixing the machines for next year.

Cities of the Columbia Plateau

In the past, most people of the Columbia Plateau worked on farms. Today, more people live and work in the cities. Yakima, Wenatchee, Walla Walla, Spokane, Pullman, and the Tri-cities (Richland, Pasco, and Kennewick) are some important cities of the Plateau. Spokane is the largest of the region. It is the second-largest city in Washington.

Researchers at Washington State University in Pullman help the farmers of the Columbia Plateau. They study farm animals, crops, and soils. They learn about better ways to run farms.
(Washington State University)

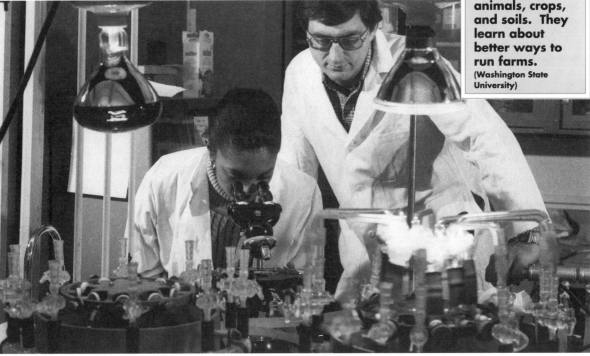

This photo of downtown Spokane shows the Spokane River and Riverfront Park. This park was the location of Spokane's World's Fair.
(Ken Olson)

Find Spokane on a map of the United States. Now look for other cities that lie between the Cascade Mountains and the Mississippi River. Spokane is the biggest city in nearly all this huge area. It has more people than any city in Idaho, Montana, Utah, Wyoming, North or South Dakota!

Spokane is an important trading center. Crops, cattle, lumber, and other raw materials are transported to Spokane from surrounding areas. Workers in Spokane's mills and factories turn these raw materials into finished products such as packaged foods and furniture. Then these products are shipped out to customers in other parts of the world. People from rural areas come to Spokane to buy things they cannot find in their small towns.

In addition to its shops and services, Spokane has beautiful parks to visit. Riverfront Park, the location of Spokane's world's fair, is a favorite.

Spokane is also a center for arts and entertainment. It has art and history museums, a symphony, and a wide range of other activities. Just outside the city are other attractions, from skiing on Mount Spokane to boating on nearby lakes.

The Columbia Plateau

Word Skills

irrigation
reservoir
dry farming
trading center

Things to Know

1. Why is irrigation needed on the Columbia Plateau?
2. What is the largest dam in the Pacific Northwest? Where is it located?
3. What is the most important crop of the Columbia Plateau?
4. What is the largest city of the Columbia Plateau?

What Do You Think?

1. Some early farmers in the Palouse Hills had the following experience: They planted wheat and did not irrigate it. The crop was good. The next year, they planted wheat on the same land, but the crop was not so good. By the third or fourth year, the crop was not good at all. Could you explain to these farmers what happened? What advice could you give them?

2. What do you suppose happens to salmon when dams are built? How can young salmon get over the dam? How can adult salmon still return to the place where they were born? Can you think of any ways these problems might be solved?

3. How do you suppose ships get past the dams on the Columbia River?

CHAPTER 20

THE OKANOGAN HIGHLANDS

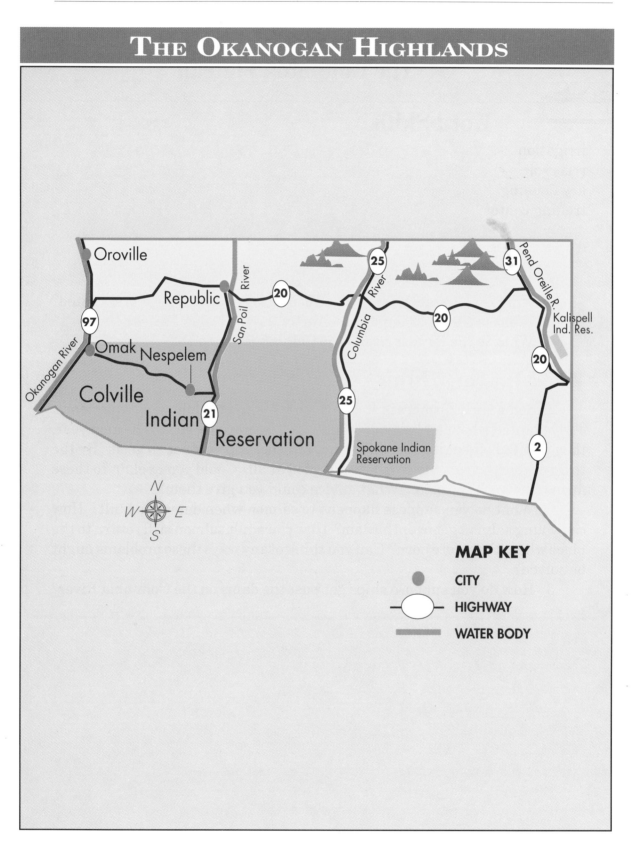

MAP KEY

● CITY

— HIGHWAY —

▬ WATER BODY

THE OKANOGAN HIGHLANDS

Highway 20 is often called the North Cascades Highway. It runs across the northern part of the state. East of the Cascades, the highway climbs up ridges and goes down through several river valleys. First comes the Okanogan River, then the San Poil, the Columbia, and the Pend Oreille. All these rivers flow south through trench valleys in the steep hills.

This area is called the Okanogan Highlands. The ridges are foothills of the great Rocky Mountains.

The Rocky Mountains

Find the Rocky Mountains on a map of North America. They stretch all the way from Canada to Mexico. They are the largest mountain range on the continent.

You have learned how the Cascade Mountains divide our state. The Rocky Mountains divide our country. The area between the Rockies and the Pacific Ocean is sometimes called the western United States, or just the West.

The roughest lands of our country are in the West. The highest mountains and the deepest canyons are here. So are the big deserts. There is more wilderness land in the West. The cities of the West are newer than most of the eastern cities. Some of the main businesses are different, too. All these differences help give western people a somewhat different way of life.

Modern cowboys in eastern Washington. How is their life similar to cowboy life of the past? How is it different?
(Special Collections Division, University of Washington Libraries)

Farms and ranches can be seen in the trench valleys of the Okanogan Highlands.
(Therese Ogle)

Western Life in the Okanogan Highlands

There are many stories and legends of the American West. You can see them in movies and read about them in books. They are stories of **cowboys,** Indians, gold mines, and wilderness. They are stories of pioneers, of people with a sense of adventure and independence.

Those stories are part of U.S. history. But they are also a part of Washington today. You can find them all in the Okanogan Highlands.

Take cowboys for example. If you think there are no cowboys left in the United States, try visiting Omak in August. This is the time for the Omak Stampede. Omak's steep downhill horse race is a famous contest of cowboy skills.

Of course, ranching has changed a lot since the old days. More than 100 years ago, cattle roamed free in eastern Washington. There were few farms and fences then. There were no roads. Cowboys grazed their herds on the open grasslands.

In spring, they rounded up the cattle and walked them to market. This was called the **cattle drive.** It was the only way to move the big animals before railroads were built.

The best-known cowboy trails were in Texas. But at one time there were cattle drives in Washington as well. The route led across Snoqualmie Pass on the old Snoqualmie Trail. It took six days to cross the Cascades.

Ranching is still important in Washington. But today, the cattle travel to market in trucks and trains. The animals live on fenced ranchland. They eat special feed grains and hay as well as wild grasses.

ROUND-UP DAYS

These descriptions of life on a round-up were written by a Washington cowboy many years ago.

"By daylight, the big camp was astir. Breakfast, consisting of coffee, baking powder biscuits, potatoes, bacon, butter, and eggs, was served by each man taking a tin plate . . . and helping himself . . .

"On the ride, several rattlesnakes were killed. . . . Several of the boys collected the rattles from the snakes killed and wore them in their hats. . . .

"Around the camp fire, one could hear many an interesting story of the range."

(A. A. McIntyre, *The Last Great Round-up*, 1906)

The children of the Spokane tribe perform traditional dances for special occasions. (National Park Service)

Native Americans of the Highlands Today

The cowboys of the West have come from several races and cultures. Here in the Northwest, some of the best cowboys were Indians!

Today, most Native Americans in the Okanogan Highlands live on three reservations. The Colville Reservation is the largest in Washington. (It once included almost all the land of the Highlands!) It is the home of several Plateau tribes. Chief Joseph's band of Nez Perce was sent here, for example. Chief Joseph was buried on the reservation.

East of the Colville Reservation is the Spokane Reservation. It is located on the Spokane River. Most of the rivers of the Highlands were named for Native American tribes. Spokane, Pend Oreille, San Poil, Nespelem, and Okanogan are all examples.

The third reservation of the Okanogan Highlands is the very small Kalispell Reservation. It is so small that it does not appear on most maps. It is located in Usk, Washington, near the Idaho border. The Kalispell culture is known for its unique form of transportation. This was the only Washington tribe that made canoes of tree bark.

Gold Towns and Ghost Towns

The Okanogan Highlands make up the smallest and least-populated part of the state. There are no big cities, but there are a few interesting towns. Many of them were started by gold miners. Oroville is an example. *Oro* means gold in Spanish.

This machine is used for mining uranium on the Spokane Indian Reservation.
(Dwight Morgan)

194

Most of the miners left long ago. But in a few areas, gold is still being mined. There is a working gold mine near the town of Republic, for example. You can still meet prospectors in this area. They spend their days in nearby mountains, looking for gold. Some of them find it! Lead and zinc are other metals still mined in the Okanogan Highlands.

FOSSILS

Not everyone in the mountains near Republic is looking for gold. Some are looking for fossils. Fossils are remains of animals or plants that lived long ago.

In ancient times, before people lived in the Highlands, there was a lake here. Leaves, twigs, and seeds fell into the lake. They left their impression in the soft mud of the lake bottom. These are the fossils you can find near Republic today.

Examining fossils found near Republic, Washington.
(© 1991 Mary Randlett)

Discovering Washington

This chapter brings us to the end of our study of Washington State. In this book, you have learned about the people and places of Washington, our government, and our history. You have learned something about Washington's place in the region, the country, and the world.

In the years ahead, you can continue discovering Washington by visiting its parks and cities, talking to people who live here, and paying attention to the news. This is our state, and you have a place in its future!

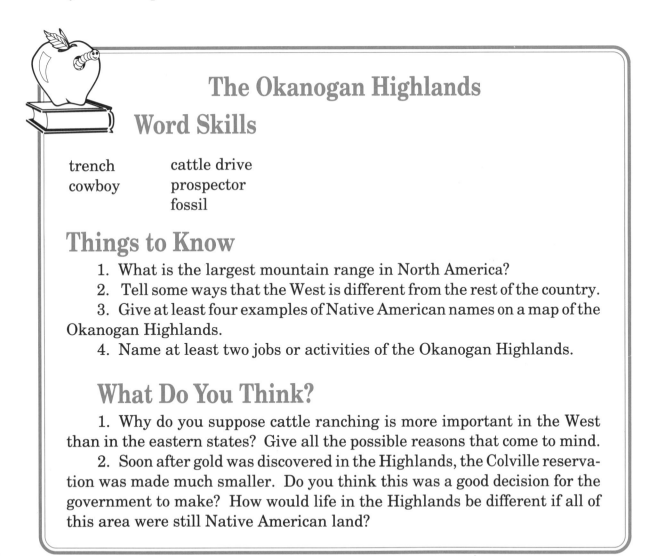

The Okanogan Highlands

Word Skills

trench   cattle drive
cowboy   prospector
                fossil

Things to Know

1. What is the largest mountain range in North America?
2. Tell some ways that the West is different from the rest of the country.
3. Give at least four examples of Native American names on a map of the Okanogan Highlands.
4. Name at least two jobs or activities of the Okanogan Highlands.

What Do You Think?

1. Why do you suppose cattle ranching is more important in the West than in the eastern states? Give all the possible reasons that come to mind.
2. Soon after gold was discovered in the Highlands, the Colville reservation was made much smaller. Do you think this was a good decision for the government to make? How would life in the Highlands be different if all of this area were still Native American land?

GLOSSARY

adapt: to do things differently in order to live in a new situation or place

Allies (AL-lyz): the countries that were on the same side as the United States during World War II: England, France, Canada, Philippines, U.S.S.R., and others

ancestor: a person who came before another person in a family, such as a great-grandfather

apology: an expression of regret or sorrow for doing something wrong

artifact: anything made by humans; often used to describe earlier cultures

ash: the dust that remains after something has been burned; tiny, dustlike bits of lava formed when a volcano explodes

atomic bomb: a bomb powerful enough to destroy an entire city. This power, along with harmful radiation, is released when atoms are broken apart.

Axis powers: the countries on the same side as Germany during World War II: Germany, Italy and Japan

basin: the land drained by a river and its tributaries, a sink or washbasin; also a large, wide valley bordered by mountains

boundary: a dividing line

branch of government: one of the three main parts or sections of government

brigade: a group of people organized to do something together

capital: the place of government; a capital city

capitol: the building in the capital city where the legislative branch of government meets

cattle drive: cowboys walking cattle to market

civil rights: rights guaranteed by law to all people in a nation

claim: to state that something belongs to oneself or one's country

climate: the average weather conditions of a place over several years

coal: a black, solid mineral that is used as a fuel

coast: the land near a shore

commute: to travel back and forth to someplace regularly

compass rose: a symbol on a map that shows direction

compete: to try to obtain the same thing that someone else wants

conflict: to disagree with someone or to fight against them; a struggle or battle between opposing sides

coniferous (Kaw-NIH-fur-us): the kinds of trees and shrubs that produce cones

continental climate: weather conditions of inland areas; hot in summer and cold in winter

continent: one of the seven very large land areas of the world

county: an area of local government, a section or division of a state

county seat: the center of government for a county

cowboy: a person who works for a ranch and takes care of cattle

culture: the way of life of a group of people—what they eat and wear; how they behave; their art, music and religion

degree: a unit of measurement

depression: a time when companies lose business, banks fail, and people lose their jobs

desert: a dry region where only a few special kinds of plants can grow

district: a specialized local government, such as a school district or water usage district

diverse (dy-VURS): unlike; differing one from another

driftwood: wood that has been carried ashore by the ocean

dry farming: raising a crop such as wheat without the use of irrigation water; relying only on rainfall and water stored in the soil

economy: a system that includes how people make their living; how goods and services are made, bought and sold

election: the process of choosing someone by voting

electronics: a science dealing with the use and behavior of electrons and electricity

elevation: the height of the land

equator: an imaginary line around the earth halfway between the north and south poles

erosion: wearing away of the land by water, wind, or other forces

eruption: the bursting forth of something, such as lava from a volcano

ethnic group: a group of people that can be classed together because of their shared race, culture, or customs

exclude: to shut out, keep out

executive: the branch of the government which carries out the laws

explorer: a person who goes to an unknown land to learn about it

extinct: no longer existing

federal: relating to the government of an entire country

flour mill: a place where machinery grinds grain into flour

foothill: a hill at the base, or foot, of higher hills or mountains

fossil: the remains or print of an animal or plant that lived long ago

general strike: many groups of workers all refusing to go to work at the same time

geography: the study of the earth and the people, animals and plants living on it

geology: the scientific study of the earth and its history, especially through the study of rocks and minerals

glacier: a large body of ice moving slowly down over an area of land

gold rush: a rush to newly discovered gold fields in hopes of becoming rich

graze: to eat grass

headquarters: the center of a business or military unit; the place where the person in charge works

Hispanic: people of Spanish or Portuguese-speaking background

hydroelectricity: electricity made by water power

ice age: a period of extreme cold lasting thousands of years; a time of widespread glaciers

immigrant: a person who goes to another country to live

international trade: buying and selling goods with other countries

internment (in-TURN-ment): to confine someone in a camp or prison, especially during a war

invention: a product or idea that is created or produced for the first time

irrigation: to supply land with water by means of canals, ditches or sprinkler systems

isolated: kept apart from others

judicial (jew-DISH-ul): the branch of government, made up of courts and judges, which makes decisions and judgements about laws

labor union: a group of workers who join together to get improvements in their working conditions

latitude: imaginary lines on the earth that measure the distance north or south of the equator

lava: molten rock that comes to the surface of the earth

legends: stories about one's beliefs or history that are passed on from one generation to the next

legislative: the branch of government that makes laws

location: the place where something is

longhouse: a house of cedar built by the coastal Native Americans where several families lived in together

longitude: imaginary lines on the earth that measure distance east or west of the prime meridian

lumber: timber or wood, especially that which has been sawed into boards

manufacturing: making products from raw materials

map key: an explanation of the symbols on a map

marine climate: weather conditions that are special to coastal areas; usually wet and mild

metropolitan area: an urban area that includes one or more major cities and their suburbs

mild: gentle; not strong or violent

miner: a person who goes into a pit or tunnel dug into the earth to take out minerals

missionary: a person sent to spread a religous faith among unbelievers

molten: melted

mountain man: a man who trapped animals for their fur; he usually worked alone

Native American: someone whose ancestors were among the first people to live on the American continents: another name for Indian

natural resource: something found in nature that is useful to people, such as coal or trees

natural vegetation: plants and trees that are native to an area, not brought in from somewhere else

New Deal: the plan of President Franklin D. Roosevelt to end the Depression by creating new laws and services and many government jobs

old growth forest: an ancient forest, including trees, plants, and animals, that has existed on its own for hundreds of years without being changed by human action

peak: a mountain that rises above others nearby; the top of a hill or mountain

peninsula: a piece of land surrounded on three sides by water

pioneer: an early settler in an area; one of the first people to do something new

pit house: a house built partly underground by the plateau people

plateau (pla-TOH): a high, mostly flat area of land

plywood: a strong piece of wood made of many thin layers of wood glued together

population: the number of people living in a country, city or area

port: a harbor where ships load and unload cargo

potlatch (POT-latch): a coastal Native American custom where the host gives presents to the guests

prairie: a large area of flat grassland with few trees

precipitation: water that falls to earth as rain, sleet, snow or hail

prejudice (PREH-juh-dus): an opinion formed before studying facts; anger or dislike toward a group of people because of their race, color, religion or culture

prospector: a person who explores for mineral deposits such as gold

prosperity: wealth; the state of being rich

raft: a flat log structure used as transportation on water

rain forest: a forest area with an average yearly rainfall of over 100 inches

region: a part of the country or an area of the world. The lands in a region have some things in common and are different from other regions in some ways.

register: to enter one's name on a list

relationship: a connection between two things

rendezvous (RAWN-day-voo): a planned meeting

representative: a person who speaks or votes for other people

represent: to speak or vote for someone else

reservation: land set aside by the government for Native Americans to live on

reservoir (REZ-ur-vwahr): a lake, tank or pool where water is stored

resident: a person who lives in a place for a length of time

sawmill: a mill or factory having machinery for sawing logs

scale of miles: a line divided into regular spaces and used for measuring distances on a map

sea level: the level of the ocean. Elevation is measured in the distance above sea level

segregate (SEG-reh-gayt): to separate a group of people from the rest because of their color, race, religion or culture

senator: a member of the senate; a person elected to help make laws

services: help or aid which governments provide the people, such as schools and fire departments

shaman (SHAW-mun): a Native American religious leader who cures the sick

similar: alike

software: the programs that make a computer work

spike: a long, thick metal nail used to connect railroad ties to the rails

stockade: a high fence surrounding a fort

streetcar: a vehicle that runs on rails on city streets

strike: workers refusing to work as a way to get higher pay or better working conditions

suburb: a community next to a large city

symbol: something that stands for something else

tax: money the government collects from the people to pay for government services such as schools, police, and roads

technology: the skills, knowledge and tools of a culture or industry

territorial government: the system for running a territory. Government leaders in United States territories are appointed by the president.

territory: land that is owned by a country, but is not a state

tide: the rising and falling of the ocean twice a day

time line: a diagram showing when important events happened

tipi (TEE-pee): a tall, cone-shaped tent held up by a circle of tall poles

tourism: the accommodating of travelers

trade: the business of buying and selling or exchanging goods

trading center: a city where many raw materials are brought in from surrounding areas, turned into finished products, and sold

trail: a cleared or marked route

treaty: an agreement between two countries

tree line: the elevation above which no trees can grow

trench valley: a long and narrow strip of land with hills or mountains on both sides

tributary: a stream flowing into a larger stream or river

urban: having to do with a city

vast: huge, enormous, great

volcano: a hole in the earth's crust which molten rock and steam come out of; a mountain or hill made up of this rock

wagon train: a group of wagons traveling together

weather: the temporary state of the air, hot or cold, wet or dry, calm or stormy

weir (WEER): a wooden fence built across a stream to trap fish

INDEX